YACHT DESIGNER'S SKETCH BOOK:

HINTS AND ADVICE FOR THE AMATEUR AND THE PROFESSIONAL

IAN NICOLSON

C. ENG., FRINA, HON. MIIMS

AMBERLEY

First published 1982, this edition published by Amberley Publishing 2015.

Amberley Publishing
The Hill, Stroud
Gloucestershire, GL5 4EP

www.amberley-books.com

British Library Cataloguing in Publication Data.
A catalogue record for this book is available from the British Library.

ISBN 978 1 4456 5150 7 (print)
ISBN 978 1 4456 5151 4 (ebook)

Typeset in 11pt on 15pt Sabon.
Typesetting and Origination by Amberley Publishing.
Printed in the UK.

Contents

Introduction   5

1   Construction   7

2   Traditional Fittings   23

3   Racing Dinghies   33

4   Spars and Rigging   47

5   Plumbing   61

6   Vents and Hatches   73

7   Deck Fittings   79

8   Engines   101

9   Cabin Furniture   109

10 Sails and Cloth Fittings   125

11 Maintenance and Improvements   139

Introduction

When I sailed a little cruiser that I'd built across the Atlantic on my own, I had no self-steering gear. It was many years before such equipment could be bought, and as I'd built the boat in a rush one summer, I had no time for making gadgets. Once out in deep water, I coaxed the boat to sail herself on some points, but self-steering arrangements are unreliable in light airs, especially if there is a lop. When a big sea is left over after a gale, a wind-operated self-steering gear is sheltered from the breeze in the deep troughs and becomes even less effective.

To get over this problem, I made a special tiller extension. Unlike the normal extension, which is pivoted with a universal joint at the tiller end, my extension was rigidly attached and reached forward through the entrance right into the cabin. I had my reserve compass recessed into the chart table by the companion steps, opposite the galley, which was the height of luxury. I was able to sit under the main hatch and steer with one hand, and either navigate or cook with the other. I could tell by the feel of the boat if I was getting too close or too far off the wind, and the compass confirmed my suspicions. The cabin steps were wide enough for sitting comfortably, either with my head in the dry just below the hatch, or on a lower step at just the right height for reading a book lying on the chart table. When it rained, I sat snugly for hours out of the cold and cooked meals of great size and succulence, steering with two fingers all the while. Every so often I looked out of the hatch to see who was going to hit me and how soon.

The extension was devised so that with the normal amount of weather helm, the forward end of the wood rod came to the middle of the hatch-way. That is, the extension, though fixed tightly to the tiller, was at a slight angle to it. When we went about I had to tack the tiller extension too, but that was a small disadvantage as I only tacked about once a week.

I don't claim to have invented this type of tiller extension because so many things that seem like new inventions turn out to be very old ideas. For instance, the Tamils held up their small boat rigs hundreds of years ago, so sail-boards or wind-surfers are nothing new. What I did find a great delight was the simplicity of my extension, and its continued success.

The best gadgets tend to have few, or better still no, moving parts. Whenever I'm developing any idea I try and make it easy enough for a youngster to make, with the minimum number of different materials, few parts and, above all, the maximum seaworthiness. If I draw out someone else's ideas I try to increase the simplicity, strength, radius of the edges, and number of applications, and decrease the weight and cost, number of corners and tools needed for the project. Above all, I hope that it will solve someone's problem.

I've been helped by a few thousand owners, crew, designers, boatyard managers, foremen and charge-hands, shipwrights and engineers, riggers and painters, fitters and boatbuilders, sail-makers and inventors. Ever since my column called 'Designer's Diary' in the magazine *Yachts and Yachting* started in 1954, I've been given permission to use ideas in the most generous way by a wide variety of people. So my thanks go to these people and to the owners, editor and staff of *Yachts and Yachting* for their help and permission to use these ideas and some of the drawings which first appeared in that magazine.

The sketches in this book will in some cases be enough for a good shipwright or engineer to make a fitting for a particular boat. On other occasions the picture will give that spark of inspiration which solves a problem. If the sketch that is needed is not in these pages, try one of the other books of ideas, like *The Yacht Designer's Notebook* or *Marinize Your Boat*. And if the problem still refuses to yield, you could even write to the author.

There are plenty of people who say that it is not owners or designers or builders who dream up these good ideas, but the boats themselves who come up with solutions. There is truth in this. I was completing a 28-footer and was worried about keeping the cabin sole clean during the weeks of work before launching. I decided to cover the sole with cardboard before starting work, but the cardboard tore before work really began. I realised that strips of carpet over the ply sole and wrapped round its edge were the answer. In practice, I found the shape of the boat made it impossible to wrap the carpet round the ply and taping the carpet down was a failure. The boat was trying to tell me something, and when I walked over the sole I realised that due to the width between the bearers, the ply was too thin and flexy for the job. So I left the ply with no covering during the building time, and when the job was finished, I cleaned off the surface dirt and glued on top a super-quality teak-faced ply made extra lovely by a coating of non-slip varnish.

In this book I've tried to stick to simple gear. Though there is plenty here for the professional boatbuilder, a young lad with nothing more than a handsaw and a hacksaw, a drill, screwdriver, chisel, plane and other basic tools can make most of the items shown. Some things need a little welding or turning, some need galvanising or machining, but with a little ingenuity it is often possible to find ways round. If there is no galvanising plant available, a steel fitting can be burnished smooth and bright, then coated with epoxy paint so that it will not rust for years. On the same theme, before welding existed, steel boats and complex ships were built by rivetting, and a rivet is a wonderfully simple gadget.

What anyone, amateur or professional, needs is the spur of determination. Years ago, when two of us were sailing across the Pacific, we were short of fresh food. We were down to tinned butter which turned rancid in the heat, biscuits a year old stored in a musty sack, and vegetables going squashy and rotten. Suddenly, right alongside, there were porpoises. Big ones! Diving and jumping almost within arm's reach of our slowly sailing yacht. All we needed was a harpoon and we would have enough fresh meat for weeks. There was no harpoon on board but in swift seconds we had grabbed a massive barbed fish-hook (made for catching sharks) and straightened it out, lashed it to a boat-hook pole, tied a light line onto the other end of the pole, and we were in business. For sheer blazing excitement, there's nothing like porpoise-spearing when the result matters ... really matters.

Ian Nicolson

CHAPTER 1

Construction

The first boat I ever helped to build was carvel planked with bent timbers, in the traditional way. I was introduced to the boat when all the frames had just been put in and all the nails had been driven through them, but before any of these nails had been clenched up. When I climbed up the ladder and looked inside the hull, there were these hundreds of bright, shiny, sharp, copper nails, all sticking inwards, making the boat like a hedgehog turned inside out.

'Right,' said the shipwright I was helping, 'just you hop in there with this hammer, and clench up all those nails. I'll stay outside with the dolly and hold the nail heads up.' (Just in case you are wondering, a dolly in shipwright terms is a steel bar with a tapered end, held against the nail head during hammering up. Shipwrights are good with the other sort of dolly too, but then they tend to be men with every sort of talent.)

For two days, with a few rests to recover, I hammered away till all those nails were burred over. During this time it was impossible to avoid falling against the unworked nails every so often, so I know what a fakir on a bed of nails feels like. This experience made me realise that though traditional methods often give the strongest or most beautiful boat, they do call for a lot of stamina. Years later I put together a much bigger boat and the hull assembly was done one day between 10.30 in the morning and 4.30 at night. Of the team of four people, three were totally unskilled and uninterested and lingered over their lunch break. The very short construction time is some measure of the way boat construction has advanced in the last few years. This quickly assembled boat was built by the 'tortured ply' method, which is akin to cold moulded wood. It consists of pulling the boat's two sides (made from long lengths of marine ply) up against pre-shaped bulkheads spaced at close intervals along the length of the boat. It is a dramatic way to build a boat and is normally faster and cheaper than methods like fibreglass, ferro-cement and other popularised techniques. It is surprising it is not used more.

The ideas shown here can be used in more than one type of construction, and can be adapted in different ways. Boatbuilders are lucky that they can learn from people who make other forms of transport, but boatbuilding is more demanding than other kinds of construction because the consequences of failure are so grim ... yet the builder rarely has much supervision and his work is seldom inspected. He needs to be conscientious.

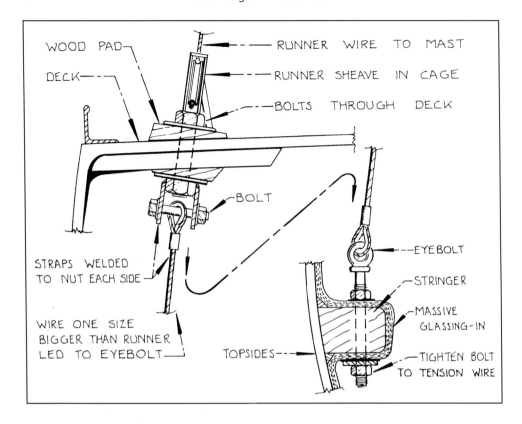

Holding down runner sheaves

This arrangement is suitable for boats of the Half Ton size and less. For bigger boats, the idea can be used but the various components will need beefing up. Where the runner wire goes round a sheave on deck and back to a winch there is a tremendous upward pull on the deck. This is contained by a wire, or pair of wires, which extend down to a well glassed-in stringer. The top end of the wire is held by a pair of plates welded to the nut which takes the bolt through the deck and through the sheave cage base flange.

The bottom end of the wire is on an eyebolt which can be tensioned to tighten up the wire. On large boats it will be necessary to fit an eyeplate with two or four bolts, and have a rigging screw on the bottom end of the wire.

Racing machine

These ideas were taken from a 26-foot (8-metre) overall length David Thomas design. The top sketch shows the forward cockpit with forestay plate down below deck level. This means that the crew are in a safe deep recess when changing headsails and the foot of the sail is right down on deck for aerodynamic efficiency, with no chance of the wind leaking under. The cockpit also acts as the forward end of the spinnaker chute.

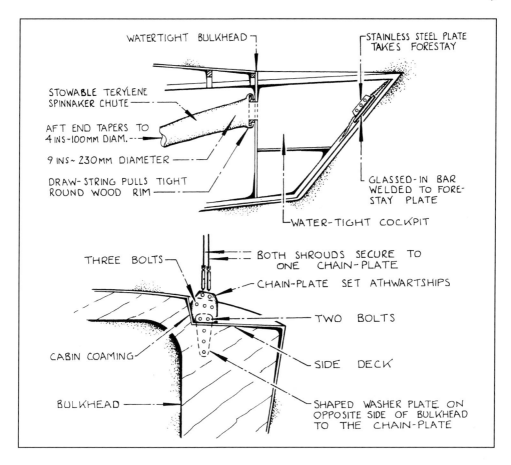

The fore deck is heavily cambered but the side decks are flatter. The change of level occurs at the mast support bulkhead. The chain-plates are secured at this bulkhead outboard of the cabin coamings, so that all the high stresses in this area are contained by this strong bulkhead.

Centreboard access (overleaf, above)

On a decked boat the centreboard is likely to be no toy. On racing dinghies centreboards are small enough to lift in and out; annual maintenance is seldom much of a problem and in any case, work on the centreboard is done ashore. On bigger boats the problem is more serious, and the top of the casing may well be only a short distance above the waterline. There will be times when access to the lifting tackle is needed; a careful crew will inspect it two or three times every season.

A Henderson hatch is very convenient for access, because it is big enough to put a hand or light through. However, it should not be fitted below the waterline because although it is watertight, it is not a good idea of have even the edge of the hatch permanently immersed.

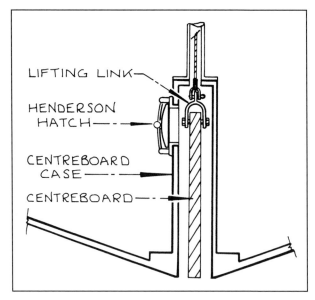

LIFTING LINK

HENDERSON
 HATCH

CENTREBOARD
 CASE

CENTREBOARD

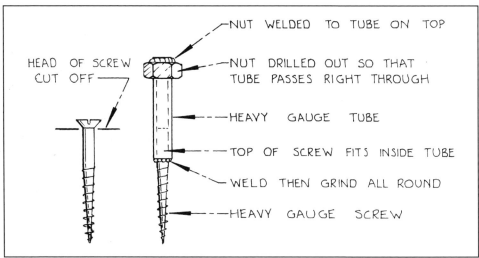

NUT WELDED TO TUBE ON TOP

HEAD OF SCREW
CUT OFF

NUT DRILLED OUT SO THAT
TUBE PASSES RIGHT THROUGH

HEAVY GAUGE TUBE

TOP OF SCREW FITS INSIDE TUBE

WELD THEN GRIND ALL ROUND

HEAVY GAUGE SCREW

Homemade super screws (above)

When building or repairing boats it is often necessary to use coachscrews, those big strong screws with hexagonal or square heads. These screws give a lot of strength (though not as much as bolts) and have a wide variety of uses. Unfortunately, they are not always easy to obtain, and sometimes those available are too short. It is not difficult to make up a special heavy duty screw using an ordinary large woodscrew, a length of tube, and a nut drilled out to fit.

   These coachscrews should not be used for holding down engine feet. However, sometimes it is impossible to get ordinary bolts through, in which case two out of four feet may be held down by this type of screw provided the engine is less than 8 horse power.

Crew protector (below)

Inside any boat there are always too many places where crew can hurt themselves and oilskins can be torn. A typical example is the nut on each stringer bolt inside a wooden yacht.

To reduce the risk of injury, some fairing piece which smooths over the obstruction is needed. For upstanding nuts a ply disc made on a lathe with nicely rounded edges is quick to make and fit. It is glued in with an epoxy resin and varnished or painted to match the stringer.

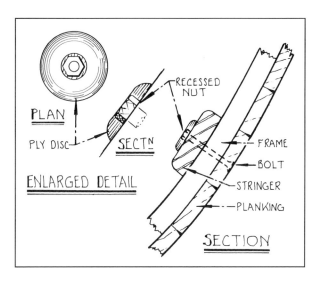

Low cost deck (below left)

It is usual to have a fibreglass deck on a fibreglass hull, but there are several reasons for breaking with standard practice. Some deck mouldings are more expensive than ply decks, and most are more flimsy. Anyone who wants a cheap deck, or a very tough one (for ocean cruising perhaps), or both these attributes, should seriously consider fitting a marine ply deck on a standard hull.

The sketch shows how the job is done quickly and at a low cost. The deck is lightly bolted at about 18-inch (500-mm) intervals all round, then the main bolting is put in through both the deck and the toerail. In this way time and money are saved. There may even be a genoa sheet lead track on the toerail, held by the same bolts, though it is more usual to have the track further inboard.

The bolts have half-hard washers against the fibreglass flange, with metal washers beneath, before the nut is put on.

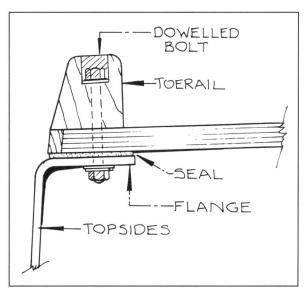

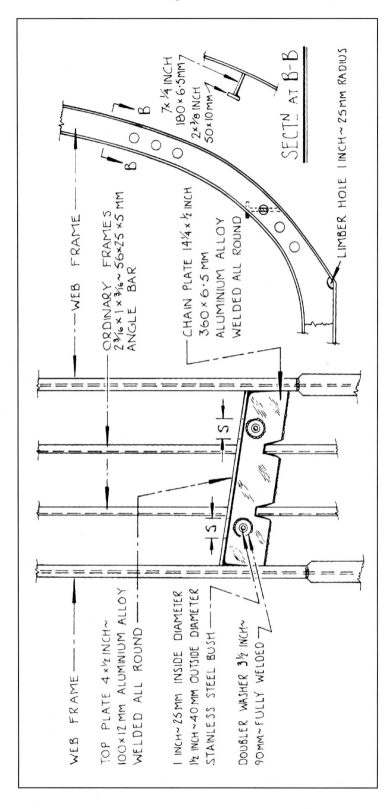

WEB FRAME

WEB FRAME

ORDINARY FRAMES
$2\frac{3}{16} \times 1 \times \frac{3}{16} \sim 56 \times 25 \times 5$ MM
ANGLE BAR

CHAIN PLATE $14\frac{1}{4} \times \frac{1}{2}$ INCH
360×6.5 MM
ALUMINIUM ALLOY
WELDED ALL ROUND

TOP PLATE $4 \times \frac{1}{2}$ INCH $\sim$
100×12 MM ALUMINIUM ALLOY
WELDED ALL ROUND

1 INCH ~ 25 MM INSIDE DIAMETER
$1\frac{1}{2}$ INCH ~ 40 MM OUTSIDE DIAMETER
STAINLESS STEEL BUSH

DOUBLER WASHER $3\frac{1}{2}$ INCH $\sim$
90 MM $\sim$ FULLY WELDED

$7 \times \frac{1}{4}$ INCH
180×6.5 MM

$2 \times \frac{3}{8}$ INCH
50×10 MM

SECTN AT B-B

LIMBER HOLE 1 INCH ~ 25 MM RADIUS

Below deck chain-plates (opposite)

On the 12-metre *Lionheart* the chain-plates are set well down inside the hull, and are in the form of T-bars welded between extra strong frames. Where the rigging screws are secured, the T-bar is cut away over the length marked 's' so that the forks of the rigging screws can slip down neatly over the double welded washers, which give extra local strength to the vertical plate. This drawing shows a number of important details, such as the way the chain-plate is cut clear of the frame to allow water to run down without being trapped behind the T-bar. The limber hole at the bottom of the frame (shown bottom right in the image on the previous page) is a good size so that dirt will not block it.

Cockpit drains on racing machine

On the 12-metre *Lionheart* the cockpit drains are arranged so that their outlets do not cause any extra skin friction. The boat is built of aluminium and the drains from the cockpit amidships run into the aft cockpit. From there, the water drains out through a pipe at each side, to cope with either tack. These pipes discharge through the stern-post plate just ahead of the rudder so that no ordinary skin fillings are involved, and the flow of water along the hull skin is uninterrupted. This technique could be copied on any boat but it has one disadvantage: there is no space to fit seacocks close against the hull shell so these important cocks have to be further up along the pipe. This means that if one of the two drain pipes fractures where it meets the hull the ingress of water will be very hard to stop.

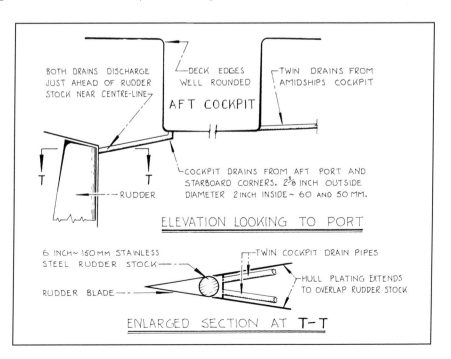

Fibreglass moulded furniture

Fibreglass furniture does not need varnishing or painting, and it is easy to clean with a damp cloth. It may tend to chip unless the edges are carefully rounded, but it has the advantage that it can be used to stiffen the hull shell. It can also be used to form the basis of other furniture parts such as the cabin sole. A detail worth noting is the way the berth cushion is held in place by a wooden fiddle. This fiddle protects the top edge of the fibreglass furniture, and gives the boat a pleasant appearance.

The moulded-in locker has several advantages: bilge water is most unlikely to dampen any clothes in it, it keeps the clothes up at a reasonable level above the bilge so that the odd sock cannot get lost in an inaccessible corner, and it is easily cleaned out.

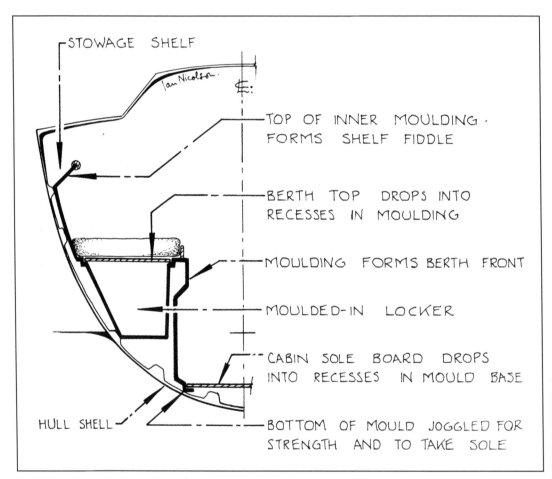

STOWAGE SHELF

Ian Nicolson.

TOP OF INNER MOULDING · FORMS SHELF FIDDLE

BERTH TOP DROPS INTO RECESSES IN MOULDING

MOULDING FORMS BERTH FRONT

MOULDED-IN LOCKER

CABIN SOLE BOARD DROPS INTO RECESSES IN MOULD BASE

HULL SHELL

BOTTOM OF MOULD JOGGLED FOR STRENGTH AND TO TAKE SOLE

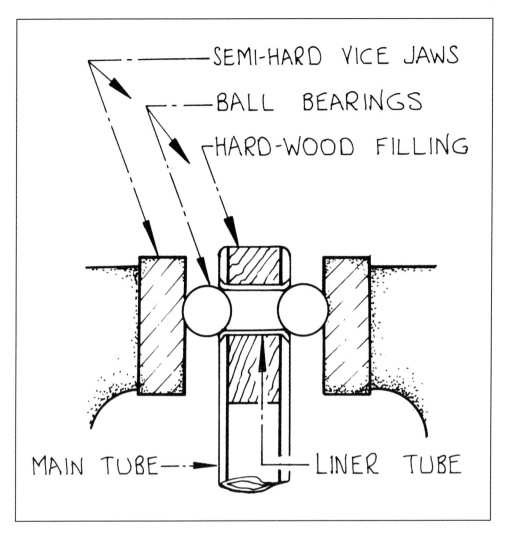

Bell-mouthing tubes

There are occasions when it is most useful to be able to line a hole with metal. For instance, when making a wooden boom the holes for reef lines, outhauls and so on will soon wear if they are not bushed with metal. Some people like to pass rigging through the ends of crosstrees instead of having the more common Y-fork ends with bolts across. Shown here is a simple method of bell-mouthing light tubes. Worn-out ball bearings are used and they are squeezed into the tube ends. In this case the main tube must first be countersunk so that the inner tube ends can be pressed into the countersunk rim. The hard wood filling is necessary to minimise the risk that the main tube will be crushed.

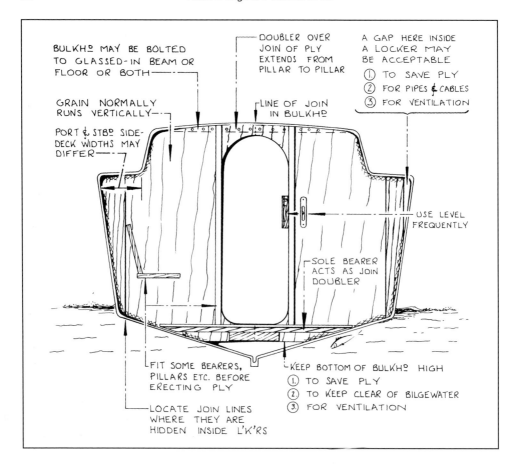

BULKHD MAY BE BOLTED
TO GLASSED-IN BEAM OR
FLOOR OR BOTH

GRAIN NORMALLY
RUNS VERTICALLY

PORT & STBD SIDE-
DECK WIDTHS MAY
DIFFER

DOUBLER OVER
JOIN OF PLY
EXTENDS FROM
PILLAR TO PILLAR

LINE OF JOIN
IN BULKHD

A GAP HERE INSIDE
A LOCKER MAY
BE ACCEPTABLE
① TO SAVE PLY
② FOR PIPES & CABLES
③ FOR VENTILATION

USE LEVEL
FREQUENTLY

SOLE BEARER
ACTS AS JOIN
DOUBLER

FIT SOME BEARERS,
PILLARS ETC. BEFORE
ERECTING PLY

LOCATE JOIN LINES
WHERE THEY ARE
HIDDEN INSIDE L'K'RS

KEEP BOTTOM OF BULKHD HIGH
① TO SAVE PLY
② TO KEEP CLEAR OF BILGEWATER
③ FOR VENTILATION

Fitting ply bulkheads

Most bulkheads in modern boats are made of marine ply. When fitting them it is sometimes a good idea to glass in a beam and possibly a floor before bolting or screwing the bulkhead at top and bottom, and glassing in all round. This technique means that the bulkhead can be put in by one person working on his own and there are no problems holding the ply up while the layers of glass harden.

This drawing shows a centreline doorway with the bulkhead in two halves, port and starb'd. To give strength at the centreline, join doublers are fitted and these should ideally be glued and bolted. The doorway pillars stiffen the whole bulkhead and add a lot to the strength of the boat. Care is needed to make sure that pillars are parallel and exactly upright both at athwartships and fore and aft.

Bulkhead panels can be stiffened by glueing and screwing, or bolting, through furniture components and cleatings to take settee bases and backs, locker fronts and so on. Where the beam of the boat is too wide for two sheets of ply, joins have to be made and these should either be covered with a material which extends right over the whole bulkhead, or they should be hidden in lockers. Joins in plastic covering material such as Formica must be very neatly made and professionals often cover joins with polished wood battens.

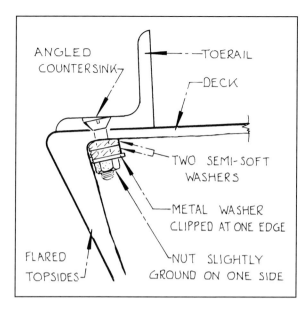

ANGLED COUNTERSINK

TOERAIL

DECK

TWO SEMI-SOFT WASHERS

METAL WASHER CLIPPED AT ONE EDGE

FLARED TOPSIDES

NUT SLIGHTLY GROUND ON ONE SIDE

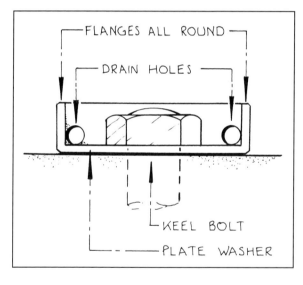

FLANGES ALL ROUND

DRAIN HOLES

KEEL BOLT

PLATE WASHER

Bolting down a toerail (left)

The technique shown here can be used in a variety of locations, quite apart from the awkward corner shown in the sketch. Bolts cannot be driven vertically down through the deck because the topsides slope in steeply. To get round the problem, the bolt hole is angled slightly and then the washers and nuts are reduced on their outboard sides to fit in the available space. The semi-soft washers can be cut easily enough but the hard washer and nut will probably have to be held up against a grindstone with a large pair of pliers. Once fitted there is no space to turn the nut, so to tighten it on the screw has to be turned from above. Before the bolt goes in it must be treated with a copious quantity of waterproof bedding material.

Keel bolt washers (left)

It is very usual to see keel bolt washers which have bent down in the middle. This results in local crushing of the wood or fibreglass and the washer is not doing its job properly.

It is not necessarily sufficient to increase the washer plate thickness by two or three times. It may still bend down as the nut is tightened.

To get over this problem, washers may be made up in the form of shallow boxes with upturned flanges all round. This gives a very stiff washer which should not cup downwards, however hard the nut is tightened.

This type of washer plate has an additional advantage in that it does not raise the height of the nut since the basic plate from which the washer is made is quite thin. If the cabin sole is right down close on top of the keel bolts, this type of washer may give just that little bit of extra clearance which is needed.

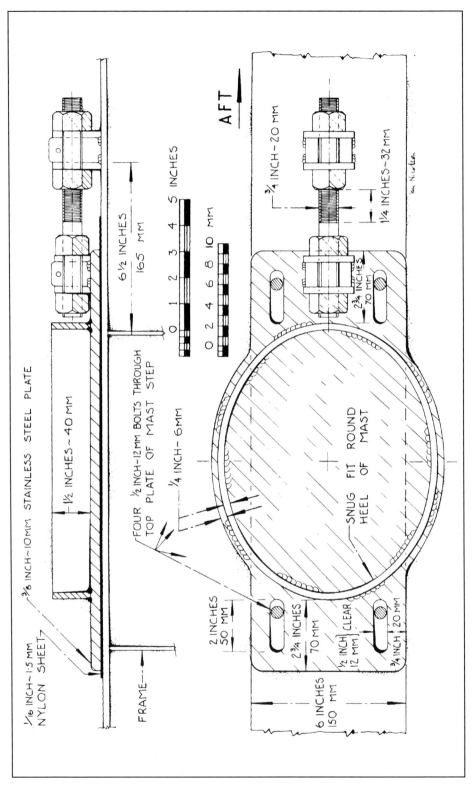

Adjustable mast step.

Adjustable mast step (see opposite)

It can be more than convenient to be able to move the heel of a mast fore and aft. For instance, if a vessel carries weather helm, the defect may be reduced by shifting the whole mast forward. Alternatively, the heel can be moved forward to increase mast rake, to help improve the tightness of the forestay, or for a relatively minor reason such as bringing the aft end of the boom forward enough to clear a permanent backstay.

This design by McGruer's of Clynder was made for a keel stepped mast, the yacht being 36 feet (11 metres) on the waterline. The fitting was made of stainless steel and it gives a travel of about 1 ½ inches. This design could be built of other materials and the fore-and-aft movement could be much greater. It is interesting to note that model yachts regularly have mast heel adjustment whereas full sized boats just occasionally do.

Among the important features which this fitting has is the powerful adjustment device in the form of a ¾-inch threaded rod, complete with nut and locking nut. With a lengthy spanner there should be no difficulty in moving the mast, although it will almost certainly be essential to slacken off the rigging at least slightly. The use of a nylon sheet is interesting because this material does tend to crush, and it might be better to go for steel plates in close contact with ample lubrication, rather than the relatively soft nylon.

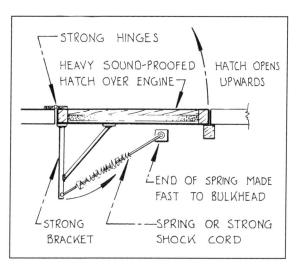

Liftable hatch (above)

Hatches over engine spaces are often very heavy, particularly if they have a lot of soundproofing material secured to them. To make such a hatch easy to open, a strong spring is fitted to it so that when the hatch is closed the spring is in tension. The spring starts at once to help the person lifting the hatch, and when the hatch is almost vertical (and therefore requiring very little lift) the spring is no longer providing much force.

This type of spring can be made from multiple lengths of stout shock cord. The amount of shock cord and the correct tension are found by experiment.

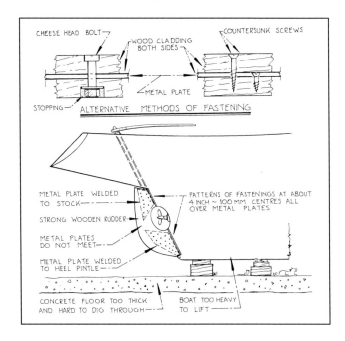

Renewing or repairing a rudder

Where a rudder stock extends up through a counter, it is sometimes impossible to remove the rudder unless the whole boat can be lifted up high or a deep hole dug under the heel of the keel. The stock has to be slid right down the full length of the rudder tube, which means that the heel of the rudder has to extend the same distance below its socket. Sometimes it is inconvenient or very expensive to dig this hole, or to lift the boat, and here is one way round the problem.

The rudder is made from a stock with a welded plate at the top, and an entirely separate plate at the bottom is welded to the heel pin. These two plates are put in place and then joined together by port and starb'd pieces of wood or ply. The wood can be joined to the plate by screws as shown top right. The first piece of wood is screwed through the plate into the wood, then the other is laid in place and screwed through the plate into the wood on the opposite side. Multiple screws spaced 4 inches (100 mm) apart are essential.

An alternative is to bolt right through the plate and the two pieces of wood at the same time.

One of the many attractions of this type of rudder is that it can be dismantled without much skill and very quickly. It can also be made wonderfully strong for long range cruising. The shape of the blade in section can be varied to suit the owner's preferences and the best hydro-dynamic theory. So that the aft edges can be well tapered away the metal plates are kept forward of the trailing edge. Where the metal plates do not occur, a filler piece of wood has to be put in, or alternatively the wood side pieces can be recessed to take the metal plate. Once the rudder has been fully assembled it can be covered over with fibreglass cloth for extra strength, and to keep out worm.

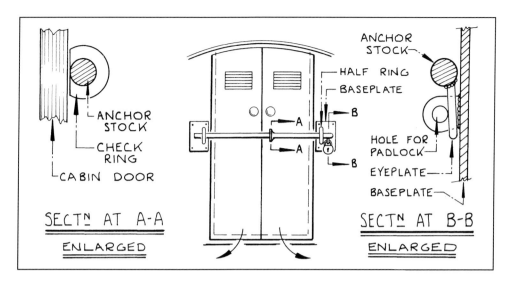

Burglar beater

If a thief approaches a boat with the idea of breaking in and then sees a massive steel bar across the cabin doors, he is bound to get discouraged and go on to look for easier prey. No one wants to carry aboard a special steel bar to fit across the cabin doors, but there is no reason why the stock of a fisherman anchor should not be adapted. The check ring in the middle of the stock will need grinding or cutting flat on one side (as shown in the enlarged section at AA) to allow the bar to fit tight against the doors.

The end of the stock which does not pass through the shank of the anchor has a loop welded onto it and this loop fits over a plate with a hole in it to take the padlock. This is shown in the section at BB on the right hand side.

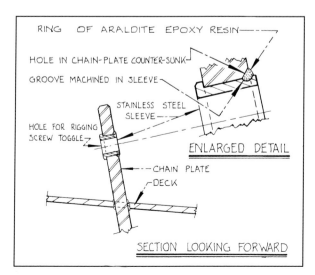

Sleeve for chain-plate

If a chain-plate is made of aluminium, the rigging screw toggle will he harder than the aluminium material. As the boat moves at sea, the hole in the chain-plate will become longer and bigger unless it is sleeved with a hard material like stainless steel.

In the same way a mild steel chain-plate will wear, and rust will show even after quite a short period at sea.

To get over these problems, a simple stainless steel bushing is needed for each hole in each chain-plate. In theory, the bushing does not need to be secured permanently in place since once the rigging screw toggle has been put onto the chain-plate, the bushing cannot fall out. However, when a boat is laid up for the winter, one or two of the bushings may be lost and for this reason it is best to have them held as shown here, using a blob of epoxy.

Sealing off a seacock hole

When a seacock is no longer needed, it is not good enough to shut the cock and forget about it. Corrosion is likely to continue, so the seacock may develop a leak when the boat is left unattended. The only safe course of action is to take off the seacock and seal the hole properly. An internal pad made from a rot-resistant hardwood treated with a rot-preventing fluid should be carefully secured on the inside of the planking. The hole is filled with a bung which is smooth and flush on both the inside and the outside of the planking.

Though this sketch is drawn for a wood-planked boat, the same principles apply to steel, fibreglass or any other material, but the internal pad will be the same material as the hull shell.

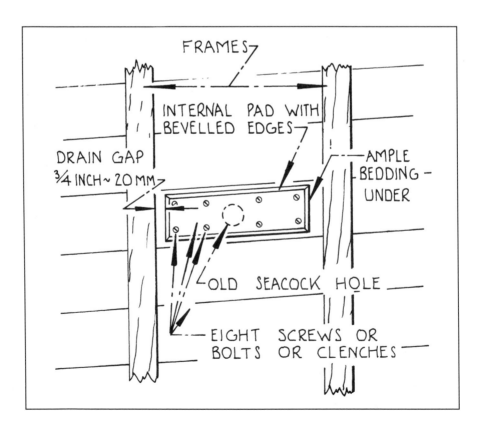

CHAPTER 2

Traditional Fittings

The history of deep-water sea-faring goes back roughly 6,000 years. In this time fittings have been developed on all the seas and on every style of boat so that by now they must be approaching perfection. There is little chance that a designer starting from scratch can expect to improve on the standard cleat, samson post or fairlead. It may be that by thought and testing and refinement someone does improve a standard fitting, but he has no right to *expect* to do so ... all the statistics of probability are against him.

That does not stop lots of us from having a go ... about ten times every year. No one is more guilty than me of trying to better the already very good ... and there is endless fun in trying, but when we think about the matter soberly, we have to admit that for a traditional need it is very hard to beat an old and well-tried design.

Changes in materials and working methods (usually brought on by new materials) result in improved gear. But not every new material is better than old-fashioned bronze or teak. So the introduction of new materials is no guarantee that better fittings will result.

This was brought home to me when I worked in a boatyard which suffered from a severe fire. Before the firemen had rolled up their hoses there were people at the yard gate inquiring about salvage. They did not want the damaged hulls, only the fine bronze cleats with teak bars and similar parts which have been so hard to find for many years. I bought four of these cleats off a superb Fife-built cruiser which was a write-off and for years treasured them till I reckoned the boat I was currently building for myself was good enough to take such fittings. One of the pleasant things about that boat was that people were forever coming aboard and admiring my teak bar cleats. It is pride of ownership that makes a boat so special, and traditional fittings enhance this pride.

Enclosed fairlead (overleaf)

This fitting goes through a low bulwark or high toerail and was originally designed for the anchor chain, though it can also be used for mooring warps. It was designed at the beginning of the century for the 50-foot (15-metre) overall length South Coast One-Design, by Alfred Mylne the First. It would be hard to improve this design, since it has no surplus weight, all the edges are carefully rounded, and it can be used on power boats or sailing craft.

Only one pattern is needed and the finished casting can be used at the bow or stern, port or starb'd. The original castings were in gunmetal and the boats were so well built that some of them were still going strong eighty years later.

A useful trick with fittings like this is to reverse them once they shows signs of wear, putting the port fitting on the starb'd side and vice-versa. However, there is ample thickness at the wearing surfaces so unless an anchor chain is let out too fast and carelessly, there should not be much wear for many years.

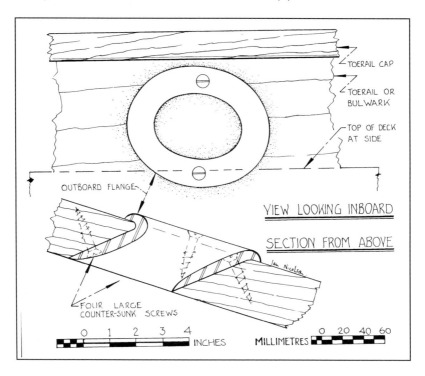

Seagoing sense from the RNLI (opposite)

At a time when so many deck fittings are being made too light, it is worth looking at some traditional fittings that were previously used on 39-foot (12-metre) Royal National Lifeboat Institution craft (opposite). At the top on the left is the design of the samson post. One of these was located forward for mooring up, or for use when the boat is being towed. There are two aft, one on each quarter, for mooring alongside or for towing other craft. The shape is carefully worked out so that it is easy to drop a loop of rope over the top quickly without any protruding horns getting in the way. In the same way, a warp can be let go quickly as soon as there is any slack on it.

The main sketch shows the protection over the hatch-way. This was built like a little low sentry box, fabricated from double diagonal mahogany all beautifully varnished, with extremely strong, well rounded, corner posts so that there were no protruding sharp edges to hurt the crew. When the hatch was thrown open, the mahogany cover was not damaged because there was a rubber stop in just the right place, and below

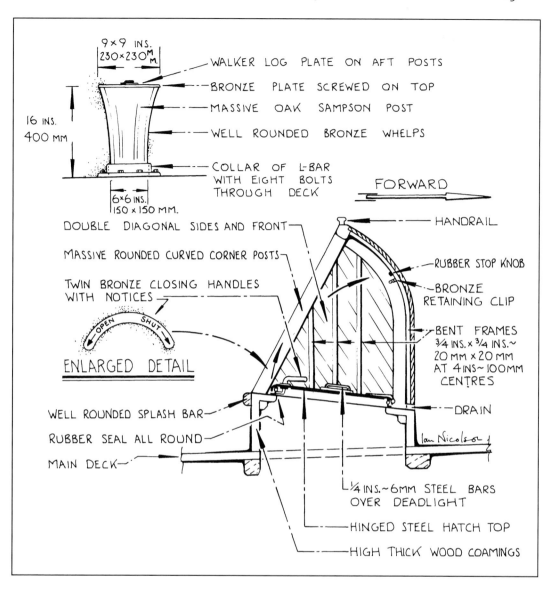

9×9 INS.
230×230 M.M.

16 INS.
400 MM

6×6 INS.
150 × 150 MM.

WALKER LOG PLATE ON AFT POSTS

BRONZE PLATE SCREWED ON TOP

MASSIVE OAK SAMPSON POST

WELL ROUNDED BRONZE WHELPS

COLLAR OF L-BAR WITH EIGHT BOLTS THROUGH DECK

FORWARD

DOUBLE DIAGONAL SIDES AND FRONT

HANDRAIL

MASSIVE ROUNDED CURVED CORNER POSTS

RUBBER STOP KNOB

TWIN BRONZE CLOSING HANDLES WITH NOTICES

BRONZE RETAINING CLIP

OPEN SHUT

BENT FRAMES
¾ INS. x ¾ INS.~
20 MM x 20 MM
AT 4 INS~ 100MM
CENTRES

ENLARGED DETAIL

WELL ROUNDED SPLASH BAR

DRAIN

RUBBER SEAL ALL ROUND

Ian Nicolson

MAIN DECK

¼ INS.~ 6MM STEEL BARS OVER DEADLIGHT

HINGED STEEL HATCH TOP

HIGH THICK WOOD COAMINGS

this a bronze retaining clip which held the hatch cover open. When the hatch was closed, daylight got through the deadlight. Even if the boat rolled right over, provided this hatch was closed and the handle locked, not a drip of water got below thanks to the rubber seal all round.

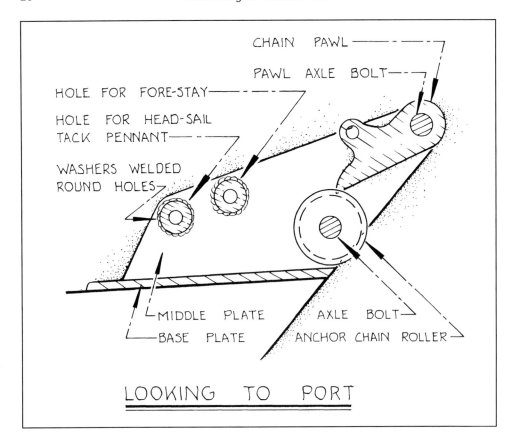

CHAIN   PAWL ─── · ─── ┐

PAWL AXLE BOLT ─── ┐

HOLE FOR FORE-STAY ─── · ─── · ─┐

HOLE FOR HEAD-SAIL
TACK PENNANT ─── ── ─┐

WASHERS WELDED
ROUND HOLES ┐

└MIDDLE PLATE   ┌AXLE BOLT┘
└─BASE PLATE   ANCHOR CHAIN ROLLER┘

LOOKING   TO   PORT

Anchor chain pawl

There was a time when lots of yachts had this simple gadget instead of anchor winches. It is a normal chain pawl located over the stemhead roller. When hauling in the anchor chain, the crew snatch in the slack as the boat dips down and the pawl holds the chain as the bow lifts on the wave crest. Much of the effort of hauling in is eliminated because it is not necessary to take the strain between heaves. For the single-hander, this pawl is a tremendous asset even if there is an anchor winch. It makes such jobs as moving the anchor chain from the winch to a mooring cleat much easier. As winches should never be expected to take the strain of an anchor chain when a boat is moored up, this change-over from the winch to a mooring strong point is important.

   The stemhead roller is shown with the starboard (near side) plate removed for clarity. The pawl is over-hung, that is, it is on a bolt end, not on a bolt between two plates. This makes it doubly important to have a very strong pivot bolt for the pawl. It is not a bad idea to make the bolt diameter ⅜ inch (10 mm) for every 22 feet (6.5 metres) of boat length.

   This sketch shows another good idea: the holes in the middle plate which take the forestay and headsail tack pennant are strengthened by having washers welded round them.

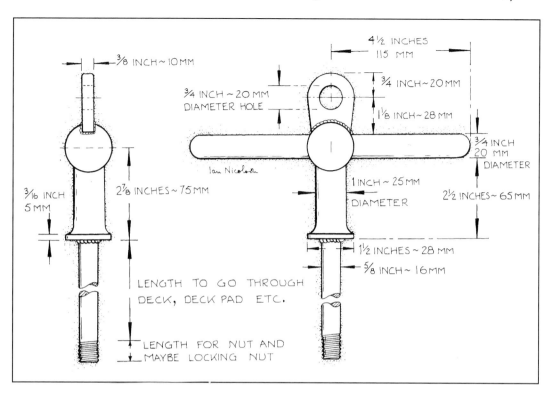

3/8 INCH ~ 10 MM

3/4 INCH ~ 20 MM DIAMETER HOLE

Ian Nicolson

3/16 INCH 5 MM

2 7/8 INCHES ~ 75 MM

LENGTH TO GO THROUGH DECK, DECK PAD ETC.

LENGTH FOR NUT AND MAYBE LOCKING NUT

4 1/2 INCHES 115 MM

3/4 INCH ~ 20 MM

1 1/8 INCH ~ 28 MM

3/4 INCH 20 MM DIAMETER

1 INCH ~ 25 MM DIAMETER

2 1/2 INCHES ~ 65 MM

1 1/2 INCHES ~ 28 MM

5/8 INCH ~ 16 MM

Tee-cleat

This is a very handy fitting, particularly at the foot of a mast. Among its many uses, it can form the base of a four-part tackle for a halliard. Instead of an expensive winch for the halliard, a hard eye is formed in the end of the halliard so that when the sail is up, the hard eye is about 3 feet (1 metre) above this cleat. The hook of the four-part or six-part tackle is slipped into the eye and the other end of the tackle secured at the hole in the top of the tee-cleat. The tackle is then pulled down tight and made fast on the cleat.

Another use is on a boat which has a halliard winch of insufficient power. In this case, a two-part tackle is secured to the halliard and the tee-cleat, and the rope if ground up on the winch, which is now giving out twice the power by virtue of the tackle. The end of the rope is again made fast on the cleat.

This particular design of cleat was done by McGruer's for a 13.5-metre, a Cruiser/Racer, a class which showed promise but never blossomed. For a smaller boat, all the dimensions can be reduced by 20 or 40 per cent according to its size.

It is important that the pull is vertically upwards. If there is to be some horizontal pull, there should be a welded plate with four bolts through instead of a single bolt at the base.

Drop down boom gallows (opposite)

Though McGruer's designed this boom gallows for a 13-metre Cruiser/Racer, the idea can be incorporated on a fitting for any size of boat. The top bar (which should always be of hardwood and ideally of teak) may have a single centre line socket, one socket on each side so that the boom clears the main hatch, or three sockets, one each side and one in the middle for use when the boom has an awning stretched over it.

When not in use, the whole gallows drops down so that the boom swings clear above it. To keep the gallows at the correct height in the lowered position, keep-pins may be slid through the vertical tubes, lodging on the tops of the flanged tubes. However, if the diagonal bracing wires are used, (and they add enormously to the strength of the whole fitting), the bottom lugs for the lower ends of the wire act as a stop and prevent the tubes dropping too far in the lowered position.

Upper stiffening brackets which hold the teak crossbar can be omitted on small boats, and the teak bar can be screwed or bolted to the vertical tubes instead.

Two ways of mounting the sunken tubes are shown: on the right, the bottom flange is carefully welded on at the same angle as the deck camber so a parallel sided wood chock is used; on the left side, a tapered chock is used underneath a horizontal flange. Another arrangement involves the use of hinged vertical tubes instead of sliding ones. If there is no room below deck for the sunken tubes, hinging is essential.

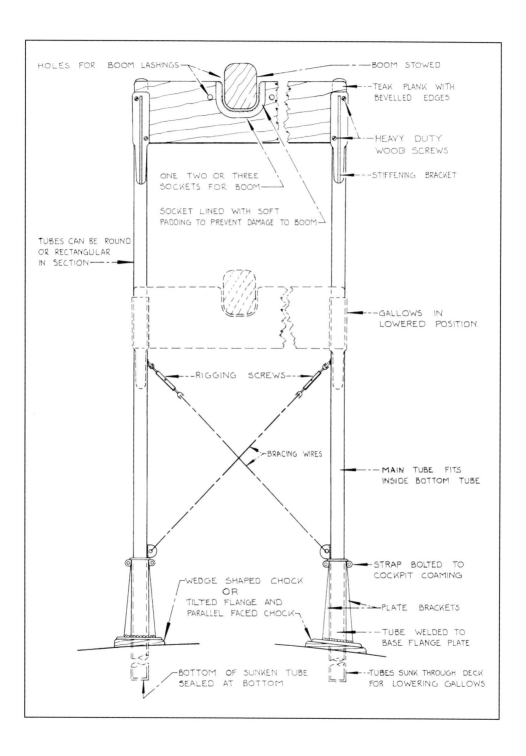

HOLES FOR BOOM LASHINGS

BOOM STOWED

TEAK PLANK WITH BEVELLED EDGES

HEAVY DUTY WOOD SCREWS

ONE TWO OR THREE SOCKETS FOR BOOM

SOCKET LINED WITH SOFT PADDING TO PREVENT DAMAGE TO BOOM

STIFFENING BRACKET

TUBES CAN BE ROUND OR RECTANGULAR IN SECTION

GALLOWS IN LOWERED POSITION

RIGGING SCREWS

BRACING WIRES

MAIN TUBE FITS INSIDE BOTTOM TUBE

STRAP BOLTED TO COCKPIT COAMING

WEDGE SHAPED CHOCK OR TILTED FLANGE AND PARALLEL FACED CHOCK

PLATE BRACKETS

TUBE WELDED TO BASE FLANGE PLATE

BOTTOM OF SUNKEN TUBE SEALED AT BOTTOM

TUBES SUNK THROUGH DECK FOR LOWERING GALLOWS

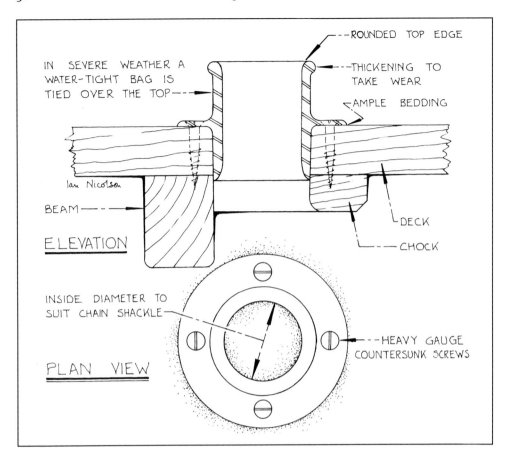

A well-tried chain pipe

This design of anchor chain pipe was produced by Alfred Mylne the First in about 1900, and it may be even older than that. Though it is shown on a wooden deck, it can be used on boats made of any material. Since there are no moving parts, (unlike the angled type with a folding lid), there is nothing to break. After a few years the edge nearest the stemhead roller may become worn, in which case the four screws are released, the chain pipe is rotated 90°, new bedding is put in, and the screws are replaced.

In this way wear takes place at a new point, so even if the chain is let out very fast this chain pipe will last many years.

The whole chain can be lowered into the chain locker with a light line made fast to the end shackle and secured round the top of the pipe, so that the chain can be pulled back on deck without going below.

If the vessel is going to sea, the chain is much better lowered right down so that its end will not bang about in the fo'c'sle. The chain pipe will be made completely watertight with a firmly lashed waterproof bag over the top.

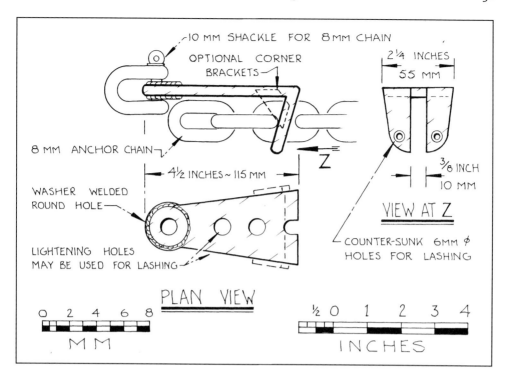

10 MM SHACKLE FOR 8 MM CHAIN

OPTIONAL CORNER BRACKETS

2¼ INCHES
55 MM

8 MM ANCHOR CHAIN

Z

4½ INCHES ~ 115 MM

⅜ INCH
10 MM

WASHER WELDED ROUND HOLE

VIEW AT Z

LIGHTENING HOLES MAY BE USED FOR LASHING

COUNTER-SUNK 6MM ⌀ HOLES FOR LASHING

PLAN VIEW

0 2 4 6 8

M M

½ 0 1 2 3 4

INCHES

Chain claw

Years ago this fitting was quite common, certainly on yachts more than 45 feet (14 metres) long. A claw is used to take the strain on an anchor chain so that the chain can be transferred from a winch to a mooring bollard.

It is most important that a boat should not be left even for a short time with the chain putting all its load onto an anchor winch. Many modern winches in particular have light weight casings and sometimes quite thin base flanges so that they are totally unsuited to the job of acting as a permanent mooring post. Each year a few of these winches fail in gale conditions and boats come ashore.

The chain claw is made of metal about 1.3 times the thickness of the chain. A claw is no good unless it is really tough. The one shown in this sketch is for 8-mm chain but the size can be scaled up for larger chains. If a smaller chain is used, the same size of claw should be used with a narrower gap between the toes of the claw. The claw is dropped over one link, and a rope tackle put on the shackle. Alternatively, a rope can be secured to the shackle and lead back to a sheet or halliard winch. Once the load is well and truly taken on the claw, the chain is quickly lifted off the anchor winch. One of the advantages of a claw is that it transfers the load swiftly and easily. The alternative is to put a rolling hitch on the chain but nowadays many crews cannot make a reliable rolling hitch, and failure here at the height of a storm can have nasty consequences.

The optional corner brackets are shown dotted. They are welded on each side of the claw as shown in plan and elevation. They add a lot to the strength of the claw.

CHAPTER 3

Racing Dinghies

I once shared an old and creaky racing dinghy with a friend. As neither of us had any money, we thought that between us we could almost afford her. She was no good in light airs, so we decided to develop her hard weather characteristics – or rather give her some, since there was no evidence that she would win in any wind strength when we first got her.

'What we need,' my friend said in that pensive way which suggests that a lot of thought has gone into the matter, 'is sheer stability in strong breezes.'

I pointed out that we both had girlfriends who were well endowed aloft and alow and would make a lot of difference to the total weight on the gunwale. I also went through the club rule book carefully and found that there was no limit to the number of people who could crew in any boat during a race.

My friend wondered how a racing dinghy intended for two people would go with four aboard, but I reassured him.

'We must have proper trials,' I said. 'There's to be none of this sloppy business of going out for an actual race and expecting to win without practice. We'll take both girls out and tune the boat.' At the time I was not sure what tuning meant, but it was mentioned in every article about racing in the yachting magazines, and it sounded good.

Conveniently it blew a near gale next week. Our girls had been warned, and they had taken all sensible precautions such as omitting to go to the hairdressers beforehand; it was obvious we were all going to get very wet and no one wants to waste money.

Getting under way proved more difficult than usual. There seemed to be an awful lot of arms and legs everywhere. And either three hands grabbed a rope when it needed pulling, or no one did because everybody thought someone else was going to do it.

At last we got the boat pointing the right way, upright, and suddenly she took off. She was scudding in a mad, breathless, broad reach before a shrieking gust. At the helm I was so blinded with water on both sides of my glasses I didn't realise one of the girls had gone overboard and the lightened boat preferred less weight. Handicapped by curtains of spray, I just peered through the murk, trying to avoid the moored cruisers all round us in the estuary.

We tore out of the side channel into the main part of the harbour, where the wind fought the incoming tide into a series of brick-shaped heaps of water. The dinghy hit

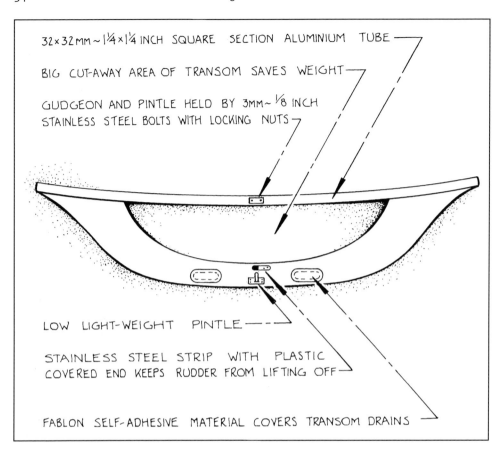

32 x 32 mm ~ 1¼ x 1¼ INCH SQUARE SECTION ALUMINIUM TUBE

BIG CUT-AWAY AREA OF TRANSOM SAVES WEIGHT

GUDGEON AND PINTLE HELD BY 3mm ~ ⅛ INCH
STAINLESS STEEL BOLTS WITH LOCKING NUTS

LOW LIGHT-WEIGHT PINTLE

STAINLESS STEEL STRIP WITH PLASTIC
COVERED END KEEPS RUDDER FROM LIFTING OFF

FABLON SELF-ADHESIVE MATERIAL COVERS TRANSOM DRAINS

the first of these and a burst of sea washed my glasses clean and clear just in time for me to see the mast go over.

'What in hell are you laughing about?' my friend wanted to know.

'We're insured,' I said. 'If we had been racing our policy would not have covered the loss of the mast. But there is no racing today, so we'll get a replacement.'

It is well known that racing dinghies set fashions and lead trends. What is done in racing dinghies today is done in larger boats a couple of years later. This makes it sensible to watch what goes on in racing dinghies to see what the future holds for every sort of boat. So far as our experiments with four aboard a small boat are concerned, the final results show no clear trend. My friend proposed to his girl not long afterwards, but mine was so upset at being left behind in four fathoms, I had to look around for another.

Modern dinghy transom (above)

This drawing shows the aft end of a 505 dinghy. However, the lessons it teaches apply to all racing dinghies and other racing machines as well. For instance, the maximum amount of transom has been cut away to reduce the weight at the end of the boat. The cut-away area has no sharp angles so as to maintain the maximum amount of strength. A strong beam extends across the top of the transom and takes the top rudder fitting, this being secured by bolts right through. The pintle has been machined away to leave just enough of the pin to take the gudgeon on the rudder.

Instead of the traditional type of hinged doors on the transom drains there is just some very thin self-adhesive plastic material. If the dinghy fills with water, this material has washed away and new pieces of plastic are put on for the next race.

Dinghy transom drains

This type of drain can be fitted not only on racing dinghies, but also in offshore racing yachts where the cockpit extends well back to the transom. The shock-cord, rope and jam cleat should also be kept well away from crew's feet. Each year it may be necessary to renew the shock-cord because this tends to perish if left out in sunlight.

The drains should be fairly well outboard so that if the boat is slightly heeled the maximum amount of water will run away. The covers can be made up of wood, aluminium, plastic or fibreglass. The ones in this sketch are of perspex machined from a thick piece complete with groove all around the rim. This groove has a glued-in soft rubber seal, and this too may need renewing after two or three years since it is likely to perish.

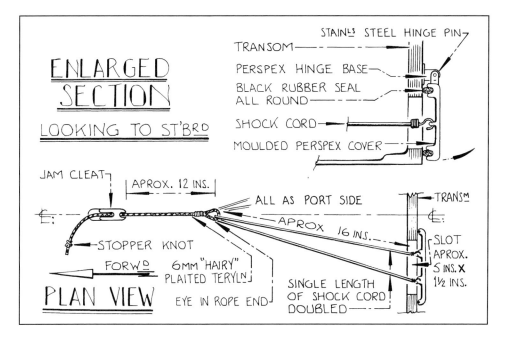

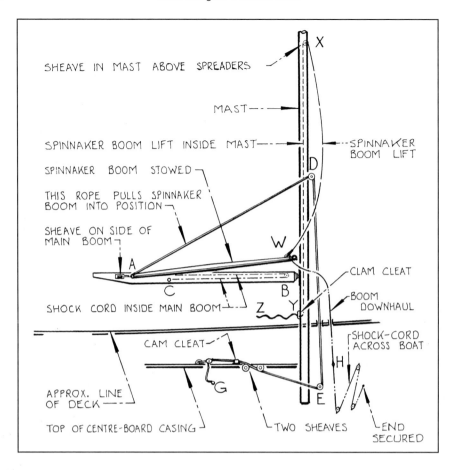

Quickly set spinnaker boom

It is not difficult to arrange for a racing dinghy's spinnaker boom to be set in seconds. The spinnaker boom is carried stowed alongside the main boom. Its aft end is held in place by a length of shock cord extending from the inboard end of the boom at A through a sheave on the side of the main boom, forward inside the main boom to sheave B and back to a fixing point inside the main boom to C. The shock cord can come out through a hole in the boom and be knotted here.

To set the spinnaker boom, the rope G is pulled and it goes via the turning block E and the upper block D to the inner end of the spinnaker boom at A. Once the rope G has been pulled tight and secured at the clam cleat on top of the centreboard casing, the spinnaker boom is in position, with its inboard end A tight up against the block D.

The height of the outer end, W, is varied by pulling on the rope Z which leads through a turning block at Y up inside the mast to a sheave above the spreaders at X. The spinnaker boom downhaul extends from the outer end of the boom at W through the fore deck to an eye H which cannot pass through the hole in the fore deck and therefore the boom cannot sky. The rope ending at H is kept tight by the shock cord zig-zagged across the boat under the fore deck.

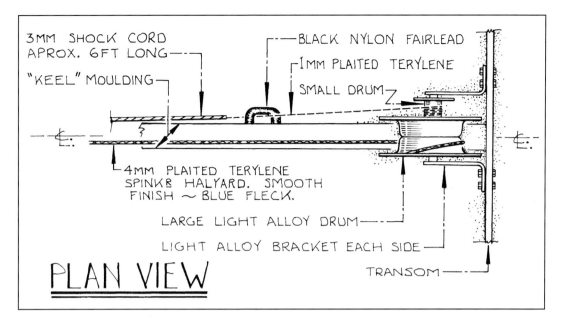

3MM SHOCK CORD APROX. 6FT LONG——·—⌐

BLACK NYLON FAIRLEAD

"KEEL" MOULDING—⌐

⌐1MM PLAITED TERYLENE

SMALL DRUM—⌐

4MM PLAITED TERYLENE SPINKR HALYARD. SMOOTH FINISH ~ BLUE FLECK.

LARGE LIGHT ALLOY DRUM——·—⌐

LIGHT ALLOY BRACKET EACH SIDE—⌐

TRANSOM——·—⌐

PLAN VIEW

Self-coiling spinnaker halliard

Though this idea is drawn out for a racing dinghy, the technique can be used on bigger boats. It can also be used for other ropes, not just spinnaker halliards.

The halliard is coiled on a differential winch, a device which is more commonly used for hauling up dinghy centreboards.

The size of the light alloy drum depends on the length and diameter of the halliard, and this can easily be worked out, either by calculation or by trial. The same applies to the small drum. The length and tension of the shock-cord will need adjusting by trial and error to suit different boats and different jobs.

Port and starb'd controls for kicker

Virtually all adjustments on any racing dinghy should be accessible regardless of whether the crew is on the port or starb'd side. This layout of the kicking strap gives an eight-to-one purchase with one end of the control line secured to each side deck.

    The two single turning blocks shown below the mast carry the rope athwartships to the side deck, but on some boats it may be preferable to run the two sides of the control along the centerboard casing and then outboard along the amidships thwart.

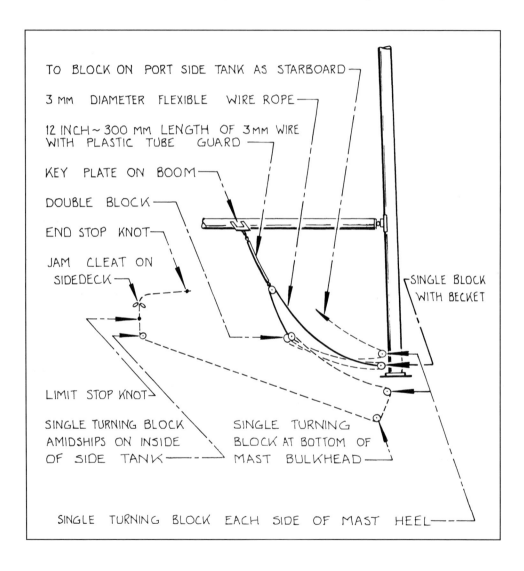

TO BLOCK ON PORT SIDE TANK AS STARBOARD

3 MM DIAMETER FLEXIBLE WIRE ROPE

12 INCH ~ 300 MM LENGTH OF 3MM WIRE
WITH PLASTIC TUBE GUARD

KEY PLATE ON BOOM

DOUBLE BLOCK

END STOP KNOT

JAM CLEAT ON
SIDEDECK

SINGLE BLOCK
WITH BECKET

LIMIT STOP KNOT

SINGLE TURNING BLOCK
AMIDSHIPS ON INSIDE
OF SIDE TANK

SINGLE TURNING
BLOCK AT BOTTOM OF
MAST BULKHEAD

SINGLE TURNING BLOCK EACH SIDE OF MAST HEEL

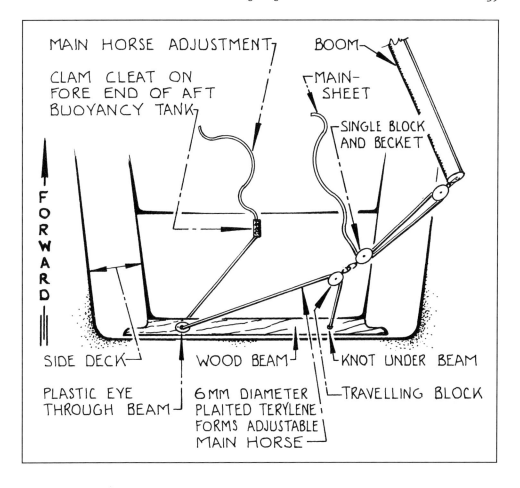

MAIN HORSE ADJUSTMENT

CLAM CLEAT ON
FORE END OF AFT
BUOYANCY TANK

BOOM

MAIN-
SHEET

SINGLE BLOCK
AND BECKET

FORWARD

SIDE DECK

WOOD BEAM

KNOT UNDER BEAM

PLASTIC EYE
THROUGH BEAM

6MM DIAMETER
PLAITED TERYLENE
FORMS ADJUSTABLE
MAIN HORSE

TRAVELLING BLOCK

Low price adjustable main horse

This main horse does not give complete control to the outer end of the boom in both a vertical and horizontal plane, but it does give the helmsman a fair amount of mainsail adjustment, and it costs very little. It could be made even cheaper by substituting a simple shackle for the travelling block, and instead of buying the clam cleat, the boatbuilder could make up a common horned cleat from a piece of scrap hardwood. He could even avoid buying the plastic eye through the beam and instead put a metal tube through the wood beam and belt out each end as shown in the chapter on Construction.

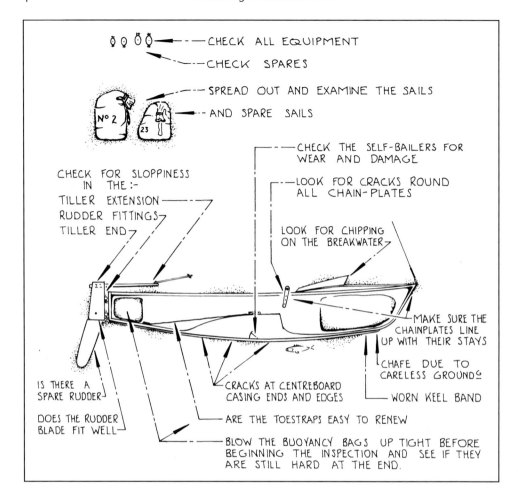

Buying a dinghy

When buying a dinghy, it is well worth while having a survey. The cost of the survey is often more than offset by the reduction in the price of the boat once the seller learns about the amount of work needed and the true condition of the craft. And if the price does not come down then the indications are that the boat is in excellent condition and well worth buying. This sketch shows the things to look for when doing a pre-survey check. There should be a full inventory of the gear and spares, and this should be signed by the seller. A clean floor is needed so that the sails can be spread out but it is better to take the sails to a sailmaker and get his opinion on them. He will be able to say if there is any more racing life left in the sails and give a rough idea of the cost of repairs.

When looking at the boat itself, it will be necessary to lie on the ground underneath the boat and a good torch is essential for a proper inspection.

Buying a racing dinghy

A racing dinghy which is out of its class has a very low value because it cannot be raced seriously, and certainly cannot be taken to an open meeting or championship. So when buying a class dinghy, its certificate should be checked to make sure it is up to date. At the same time, the owner should prove that he actually is the owner since there are too many stolen dinghies about. It is no bad thing to use a proper yacht 'Bill of Sale' when completing a purchase because this normally gives the buyer clear ownership.

The boat should be examined all over to make sure that fittings are properly secured in place, and the boat has not been roughly treated. Signs of damage on the hull are an indication that the owner is careless and there may be hidden defects, probably as numerous as the visible ones.

A powerful torch is needed when looking inside lockers and buoyancy tanks, but even better is a wandering lead because it gives a more powerful light.

Any fittings which are damaged or worn should be carefully examined with a magnifying glass because they often have a maker's number on them, and this makes it easy to get an exact replacement which will fit the existing fastenings.

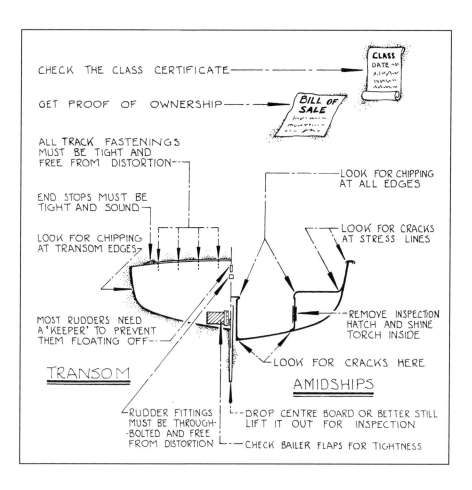

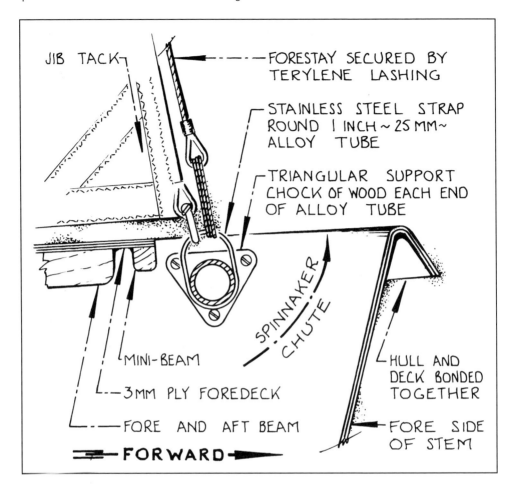

JIB TACK

FORESTAY SECURED BY TERYLENE LASHING

STAINLESS STEEL STRAP ROUND 1 INCH ~ 25 MM ~ ALLOY TUBE

TRIANGULAR SUPPORT CHOCK OF WOOD EACH END OF ALLOY TUBE

SPINNAKER CHUTE

MINI-BEAM

3MM PLY FOREDECK

FORE AND AFT BEAM

FORWARD

HULL AND DECK BONDED TOGETHER

FORE SIDE OF STEM

Unusual bow fitting

This forestay fitting was seen on an inexpensive racing dinghy. A stainless strap around an aluminium alloy tube is set back from the stem so that the spinnaker can be sent up through the opening in the deck ahead of the tube. For economy, the forestay is secured by a Terylene lashing instead of a rigging screw and the beauty of this whole arrangement is that an amateur could make up all the parts at little cost. If the stainless steel strap is eliminated, then the forestay must be secured around the tube by a Terylene lashing which will have an extra loop to take the jib tack.

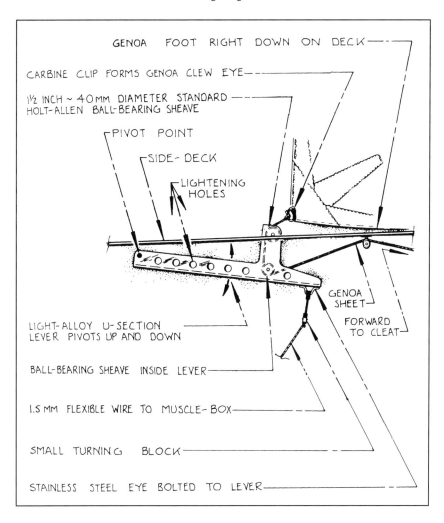

GENOA FOOT RIGHT DOWN ON DECK
CARBINE CLIP FORMS GENOA CLEW EYE
1½ INCH ~ 40mm DIAMETER STANDARD
HOLT-ALLEN BALL-BEARING SHEAVE
PIVOT POINT
SIDE-DECK
LIGHTENING HOLES
LIGHT-ALLOY U-SECTION
LEVER PIVOTS UP AND DOWN
BALL-BEARING SHEAVE INSIDE LEVER
1.5 MM FLEXIBLE WIRE TO MUSCLE-BOX
SMALL TURNING BLOCK
STAINLESS STEEL EYE BOLTED TO LEVER
GENOA SHEET
FORWARD TO CLEAT

Headsail sheeting with accuracy

This sheet lead arrangement is basically very simple, but it has many advantages. When the pivoting lever is in the down position the foot of the sail is tight down on deck and no wind can escape beneath it. Also the leech is held tight, and the gap between the headsail and the mainsail is minimised.

By slacking off the 1 ½ mm flexible wire, the clew is raised and the leech opens out giving a bigger gap between the headsail and the mainsail. This pivoting lever has all the advantages of a genoa sheet lead track and carriage with the added asset that the height of the clew can be varied from minute to minute. With a carriage on a track it can be quite difficult, and sometimes impossible, to slide the carriage forward or aft once the sail has been hauled tight in.

Though this fitting was designed for a large racing dinghy it can be adapted for small dinghies or boats up to the Half Ton size or even bigger.

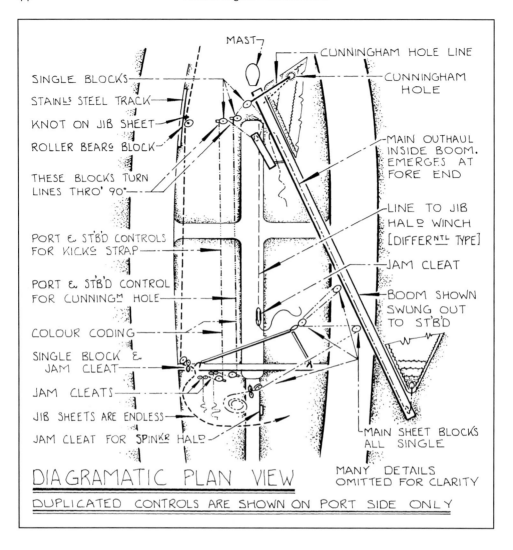

SINGLE BLOCKS

STAINLS STEEL TRACK

KNOT ON JIB SHEET

ROLLER BEARG BLOCK

THESE BLOCKS TURN
LINES THRO' 90°

PORT & STB'D CONTROLS
FOR KICKG STRAP

PORT & STB'D CONTROL
FOR CUNNINGM HOLE

COLOUR CODING

SINGLE BLOCK &
   JAM CLEAT

JAM CLEATS

JIB SHEETS ARE ENDLESS

JAM CLEAT FOR SPINKR HALD

MAST

CUNNINGHAM HOLE LINE

CUNNINGHAM
   HOLE

MAIN OUTHAUL
INSIDE BOOM.
EMERGES AT
FORE END

LINE TO JIB
HALD WINCH
[DIFFERNTL TYPE]

JAM CLEAT

BOOM SHOWN
SWUNG OUT
TO ST'B'D

MAIN SHEET BLOCKS
ALL SINGLE

DIAGRAMATIC PLAN VIEW

MANY DETAILS
OMITTED FOR CLARITY

DUPLICATED CONTROLS ARE SHOWN ON PORT SIDE ONLY

Racing dinghy lay-out

There are many ways of arranging the running rigging in a racing dinghy. This sketch shows a popular layout which applies to a wide range of types and classes of dinghy. Apart from the main sheet which is not duplicated, all the other ropes are drawn for the port side only in the sketch but must be repeated on the starb'd side.

A feature of this layout is that helmsman and crew can adjust the controls without moving from the side deck, regardless of which side of the boat they are sitting. Also, though the ropes seem to be numerous to a beginner, they are bunched out of the way for the most part. For instance, the jib sheets are much closer to the inboard side of the side deck than is apparent from the sketch. In the same way the controls for the kicking-strap and Cunningham hole are hard up against the centreboard casing, leaving the whole cockpit area free for the crew's feet.

Dinghy toestraps (below)

Some toestraps are secured by bolts or even self-tapping screws at each end. This is not satisfactory because toestraps need renewing every two or three seasons, and sometimes more often, since they chafe at certain points, notably at the ends. A broken toestrap means a ducked crew, a capsized boat, and perhaps a lost race.

The toestraps in this drawing are easily renewable and adjustable. Ideally the buckle should be kept well up by the thwart and it should have rounded edges so that no one is hurt on it. The two bands aft of the buckle keep the surplus length of strap tidy and out of everyone's way.

The height of the toestrap is critical and it can be adjusted at the ends and in the middle. It will sometimes be necessary to try the boat out several times before the final height and tension of the toestrap is just right for a particular crew.

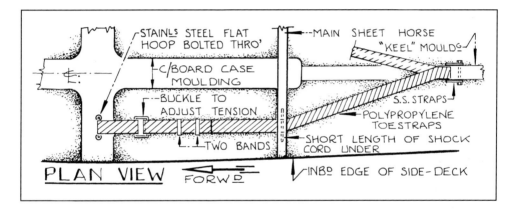

Not just for Flying Dutchmen (overleaf)

This sketch (overleaf) shows the deck plan of a successful Flying Dutchman but, as so often happens, the good idea can be transferred to other types of small boat. For instance, the bottom stiffeners and the keel are glued in to make the bottom rigid but they also give a foot grip. The keel is tapered away and is integral with the centreboard casing so that there is no 'hard spot' at the aft end of the casing.

The whole of the forward part of the cockpit is raised to make sure water quickly flows off it down to the aft well where four self-bailers quickly clear away the bilge water. By having the aft two outboard, they work even if the boat is heeled and it is noteworthy that the forward bailers are not in line with the aft ones to give a clear trouble-free flow of water past all the bailers and help them work efficiently.

Weight is concentrated near amidships. The anchor is lashed down where it will do least harm to the performance of the boat; by wrapping it in a little sail bag its sharp edges will not hurt the crew.

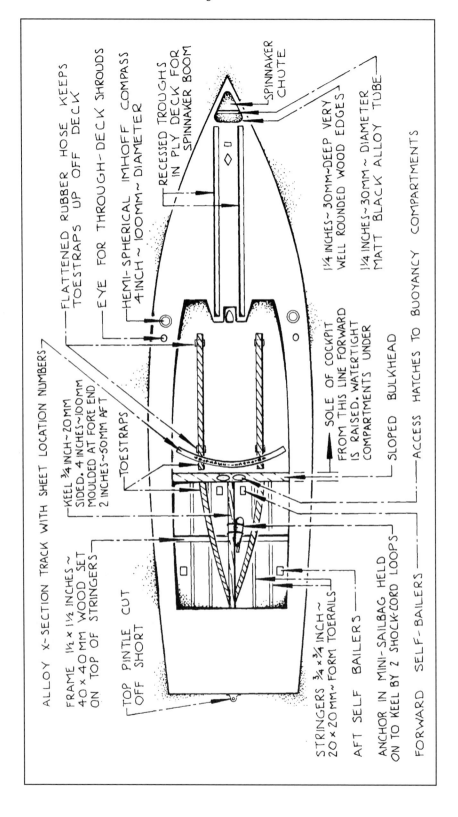

ALLOY X-SECTION TRACK WITH SHEET LOCATION NUMBERS

FRAME 1½ × 1½ INCHES ~ 40 × 40 MM WOOD SET ON TOP OF STRINGERS

TOP PINTLE CUT OFF SHORT

STRINGERS ¾ × ¾ INCH ~ 20 × 20 MM ~ FORM TOERAILS

AFT SELF BAILERS

ANCHOR IN MINI-SAILBAG HELD ON TO KEEL BY 2 SHOCKCORD LOOPS

FORWARD SELF-BAILERS

FLATTENED RUBBER HOSE KEEPS TOESTRAPS UP OFF DECK

EYE FOR THROUGH-DECK SHROUDS

HEMI-SPHERICAL IMHOFF COMPASS 4 INCH ~ 100MM ~ DIAMETER

RECESSED TROUGHS IN PLY DECK FOR SPINNAKER BOOM

SPINNAKER CHUTE

KEEL ¾ INCH ~ 20MM SIDED. 4 INCHES ~ 100MM MOULDED AT FORE END 2 INCHES ~ 50MM AFT

TOESTRAPS

SOLE OF COCKPIT FROM THIS LINE FORWARD IS RAISED. WATERTIGHT COMPARTMENTS UNDER

SLOPED BULKHEAD

ACCESS HATCHES TO BUOYANCY COMPARTMENTS

1¼ INCHES ~ 30MM ~ DEEP VERY WELL ROUNDED WOOD EDGES

1¼ INCHES ~ 30MM ~ DIAMETER MATT BLACK ALLOY TUBE

CHAPTER 4

Spars and Rigging

Most spars these days are made of aluminium alloys. These materials are easy to work, and it is surprising that more yards and amateurs do not make or repair spars. Perhaps the established spar-makers offer such a good service that it is best to go to them for every sort of help.

I've made my own alloy over the years. I was making the mast for a 41-footer I was building one summer, and, as bad luck would have it, the weather was perfect. Everybody out sailing, so the yard where the job was being done was totally deserted at the weekend. When I came to try and put the two massive lengths of tube together to make up the mast length, I needed help badly. After I had tried to do the job on my own for some time, a man wandered into the yard.

'Can you tell me anything about this yachting?' he asked.

'Yes', I said, grabbing the opportunity, 'just catch hold of the end of this long tube, that's right, now lift it, now swing round to your right, bit more, right now while I hold this end you push your end ...'

Four and a half hours later I let him go. I never did find out his surname, but he was called George, and if he ever reads this I wish to tell him that he did a great job. The mast still stands through gale and storm, just as straight and as true as we made it that long sweaty hot day. I hope your blisters have healed. And is your sore back any better? No, mine still gives me a bit of trouble, but my cut hand has healed nicely.

At least George did find out that there is a lot of interest and excitement in making spars, but it can be grinding hard work, especially when the holes have to be drilled by hand. It is like a lot of boat-building jobs: if it is tough, the satisfaction at the end is all the greater. But it does help to have mechanical tools, and sharp ones. Was it one or two hours that George and I had to plug away with those two metal files? Funny that I should have forgotten. At the time it seemed so hellish.

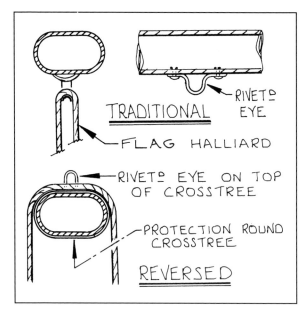

TRADITIONAL EYE

FLAG HALLIARD

RIVETᵈ EYE ON TOP OF CROSSTREE

PROTECTION ROUND CROSSTREE

REVERSED

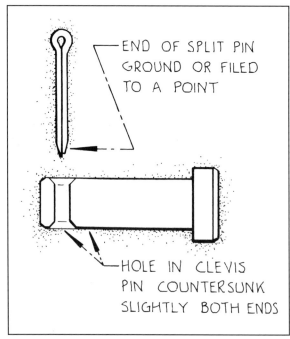

END OF SPLIT PIN GROUND OR FILED TO A POINT

HOLE IN CLEVIS PIN COUNTERSUNK SLIGHTLY BOTH ENDS

Flag halliards on crosstrees (left)

It is usual to fly flags from halliards which are fitted below crosstrees. Light riveted eyes, normally with only one rivet each side are secured on the underside of the crosstrees to take the flag halliard. It does not take much of an accident to break one of these two rivets and the halliard comes tumbling down.

A better technique is to have the riveted eye on top of the crosstree so that the halliard passes right round the top of the crosstree and is kept in position by the eye, which otherwise has no work to do. Since this type of halliard is not used a great deal, the wear on the crosstree will be minimal. Anyone worried about this wear can protect the tube of the crosstree with an extra layer of thin aluminium plating, tufnol or some similar material.

Improving clevis pins (left)

The split pin which fits in the end of a clevis pin should be a close push fit. In practice this may mean that whoever is rigging the boat has quite a problem getting the split pins into the holes in the ends of the clevis pins. Often the work has to be done aloft, in the rain, or in the gloaming.

Life can be made much easier if the split pins are all slightly pointed, and the holes in the clevis pins all countersunk just a little. This is the sort of job that can be done during a quiet spell in the winter to help ease the spring fitting out rush.

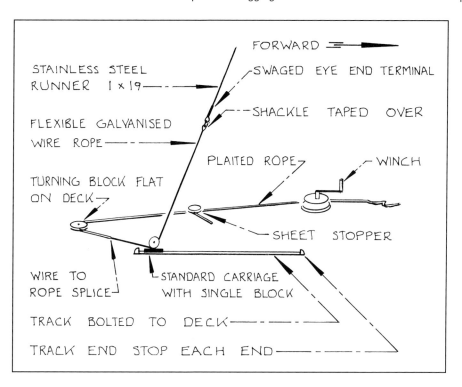

Modern runners

This layout for adjusting runners has all sorts of advantages: each part is easy to renew without replacing any other part; each part can be seen so that wear is not allowed to accumulate and by varying the tension on the winch, the rig is adjusted to suit wind speed and direction. Naturally every part must be good and strong, with substantial bolts through the deck and through underdeck reinforcing. It is advisable to put a knot in the plaited rope so that this rope cannot run out too far. It is a good idea to mark the plaited rope with coloured ink or stitched through cotton to show the crew how far the rope should be tightened.

Super simple safety (overleaf, above)

It is well known that most shackle pins are lost overboard before they wear out. One way of preventing a shackle pin from being lost is to prevent it coming right out of the shackle. This can be done by wrapping an elastic band around the pin just beyond the threaded section. A small elastic band wrapped two or three times round should be used. If a big elastic band is used it is likely to get pinched when the load comes on the shackle, and it will also prevent the shackle pin from being withdrawn sufficiently whenever the shackle has to be taken off.

The elastic band should be renewed before it perishes.

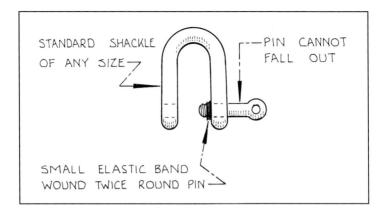

Stowing the inner forestay (below)

An inner forestay is a most useful piece of standing rigging. It is handy in bad weather to give the mast some extra support, and to take a storm jib. When the crew are working on the fore deck it is a most valuable extra hand-hold. It makes the rig more flexible because a sail can be run up the inner forestay before taking one off the outer forestay. When coming up to mooring under sail it is valuable in many boats and essential in some to have a headsail set to keep full control. But a headsail on the outer forestay gets in the way of anybody working an anchor or picking up a mooring.

However, an inner forestay is not always a complete asset. For instance, when short tacking up a narrow channel it gets in the way and makes sheet handling much harder work. Plenty of owners like an inner forestay which they can remove as required. They stow it at the foot of the mast and the neat way of doing this is shown here. The curved stainless steel plate will not damage the wire and this is most important because a kink or nick in a piece of standing rigging will reduce its strength seriously.

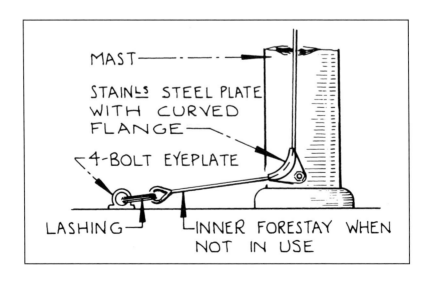

Adjustable permanent backstay

The arrangement shown here is suitable for boats up to about 33 feet (10 metres) in length. It gives quick, powerful and easy adjustment to the permanent backstay so that mast bend can be increased or decreased even by the weakest member of the crew. Each tackle should have a safety knot in it so that it cannot become unrove by accident. But even so, the backstay will not totally fail if one of the tackles is let off completely by accident.

The backstay need not be made to a very precise length, which is an incidental advantage of this arrangement. It can be fitted on counter stern boats even though it is shown on a transom stern boat in the picture. The differential lever may be of galvanised steel for cheapness, polished or stainless steel for elegance, aluminium for lightness, or titanium for millionaires.

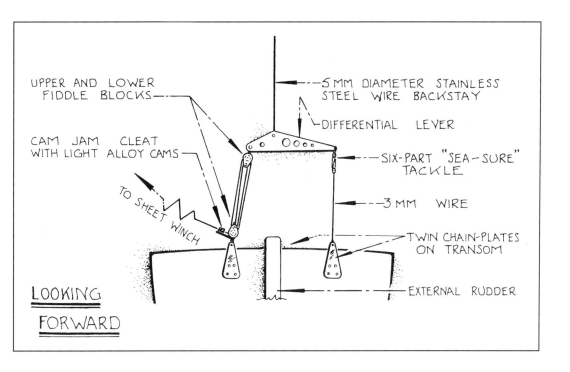

UPPER AND LOWER
FIDDLE BLOCKS

CAM JAM CLEAT
WITH LIGHT ALLOY CAMS

TO SHEET WINCH

5 MM DIAMETER STAINLESS STEEL WIRE BACKSTAY

DIFFERENTIAL LEVER

SIX-PART "SEA-SURE" TACKLE

3 MM WIRE

TWIN CHAIN-PLATES ON TRANSOM

EXTERNAL RUDDER

LOOKING FORWARD

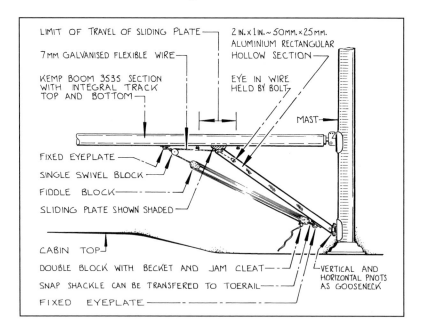

LIMIT OF TRAVEL OF SLIDING PLATE — 2 IN. x 1 IN. ~ 50MM. x 25MM. ALUMINIUM RECTANGULAR HOLLOW SECTION — 7MM GALVANISED FLEXIBLE WIRE — KEMP BOOM 3535 SECTION WITH INTEGRAL TRACK TOP AND BOTTOM — EYE IN WIRE HELD BY BOLT — MAST — FIXED EYEPLATE — SINGLE SWIVEL BLOCK — FIDDLE BLOCK — SLIDING PLATE SHOWN SHADED — CABIN TOP — DOUBLE BLOCK WITH BECKET AND JAM CLEAT — SNAP SHACKLE CAN BE TRANSFERED TO TOERAIL — FIXED EYEPLATE — VERTICAL AND HORIZONTAL PIVOTS AS GOOSENECK

Rigid kicking strap

This type of kicker was probably invented by Kemps but it can be fitted on any boom which has a strong track along the bottom. The sketch shows the size of equipment suitable for a boat about 36 feet (11 metres) overall but it is quite easy to scale up or down for different sizes.

The four part tackle aft of the aluminium kicking strap gives fine control quickly. Those two screw plates which limit the travel of the sliding plate on the underside of the boom are important since they prevent the boom rising too high if the tackle fails or has not been secured; they also prevent the boom dropping too far when the sail is lowered and a boat with this kind of kicking strap does not need a topping lift. What is important is that the vertical axis of the bottom end fitting on the kicking strap is exactly in line with the vertical axis of the gooseneck.

Removable lifelines, inexpensive style (drawings 1–4 opposite)

It can be a great nuisance if lifelines cannot be removed, particularly when a boat is laid up in the winter. End fittings for lifelines are not expensive, but the technique shown here is even cheaper and it allows the wires to be taken off easily. In the top sketch, the plastic tube has been slipped over the end of the lifeline after the latter has passed through the last stanchion. The wire lifeline is then bent round a thimble and a temporary seizing is put in place. At this stage it is often worthwhile putting on the rigging screw or end lashing so that the lifeline is pulled fairly tight and horizontal, and is easier to work on.

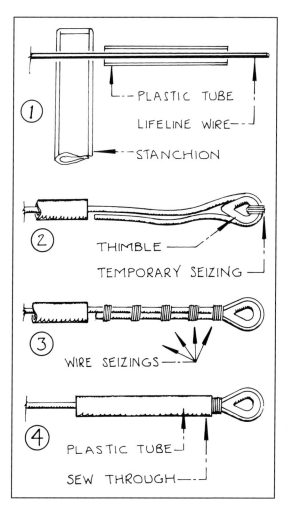

① PLASTIC TUBE
LIFELINE WIRE
STANCHION

② THIMBLE
TEMPORARY SEIZING

③ WIRE SEIZINGS

④ PLASTIC TUBE
SEW THROUGH

Five or more short tight wire seizings are now put on as shown in sketch number 3. These seizings should be twisted up very tight so that each one bites into the plastic sheathing on the lifeline. At this stage, the lifeline rigging screws or lashing should be drawn up extremely tight to check that the seizings do not slip. Finally, the plastic tube is slipped over the seizings to make a neat finish; to keep the tube in place it is sewn through once or twice.

Safe shackle (bottom left)

The type of long jawed shackle which is often used on main halliards, and sometimes on jib halliards because of its quick snap action, has one great disadvantage. The shackle is liable to drop out of the eye in the halliard, particularly when the crew are working on a plunging wind-swept deck. All that is needed to make the shackle safe is a tight mousing across the top of the shackle. The mousing must be near the curved end of the shackle otherwise the headboard of the mainsail will not fit between the jaws.

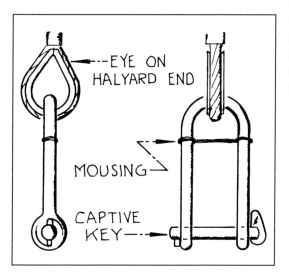

EYE ON HALYARD END

MOUSING

CAPTIVE KEY

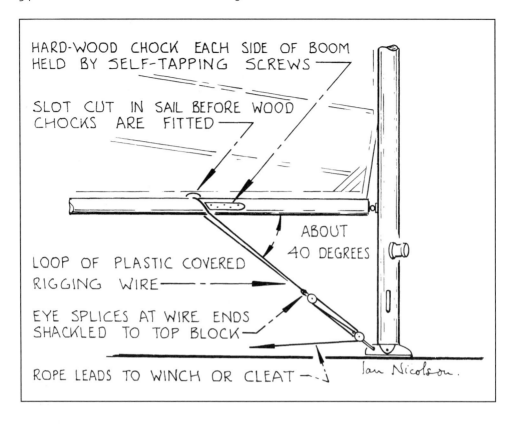

HARD-WOOD CHOCK EACH SIDE OF BOOM
HELD BY SELF-TAPPING SCREWS

SLOT CUT IN SAIL BEFORE WOOD
CHOCKS ARE FITTED

ABOUT
40 DEGREES

LOOP OF PLASTIC COVERED
RIGGING WIRE

EYE SPLICES AT WIRE ENDS
SHACKLED TO TOP BLOCK

ROPE LEADS TO WINCH OR CLEAT

Ian Nicolson.

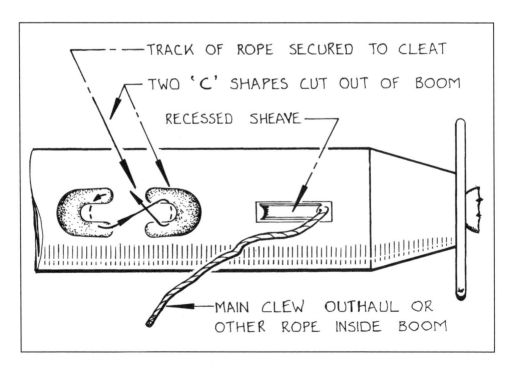

TRACK OF ROPE SECURED TO CLEAT

TWO 'C' SHAPES CUT OUT OF BOOM

RECESSED SHEAVE

MAIN CLEW OUTHAUL OR
OTHER ROPE INSIDE BOOM

Holding a kicking strap (opposite, top)

The point where a kicking strap is secured to a boom is often a source of trouble. Light metal fittings riveted on the bottom of the boom seldom last long. Cast slides fitted in the track on the underside of the boom cannot stand up to shock loadings. Some booms have no arrangement for a kicking strap and the technique shown here is good in many circumstances. A loop of plastic-covered flexible wire is made with an eye splice at each end. With a hot knife, a slot is cut in the mainsail's foot and the wire passed through this hole and doubled round the boom. To stop the wire sliding forward hardwood chocks are screwed onto the boom using a minimum of five screws in each chock.

The advantages of this arrangement are that it is cheap, quickly fitted, and can be put onto almost any type of boom with the minimum of tools.

Unobstrusive cleat (opposite, bottom)

All sorts of ropes are passed down inside aluminium booms. These include mainsail outhauls, reefing lines and so on. These ropes emerge at the forward end of the boom and have then to be made fast. If a cleat is secured to the boom at this point it is obtrusive. An ingenious way to get a securing point is to cut two C-shaped slots in the boom leaving horns pointing forward and aft which act as a cleat. Naturally the work must be done carefully so as not to take away too much metal and weaken the boom and all the exposed edges should be carefully rounded and smoothed to prevent the rope being chafed. This idea only works if the rope is relatively small compared with the diameter of the boom.

All weather main sheet (below)

In light weather, the main sheet shown on the left hand side will suit a wide range of boats. No one needs a great deal of purchase to pull the boom in, and the fewer the blocks the better when easing the mainsail off.

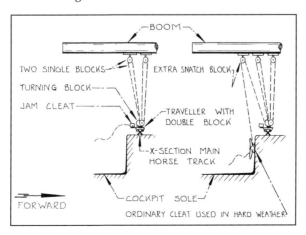

Once conditions get rough it is extremely handy if there is an extra snatch block to give additional purchase. The jam cleat may be a little unreliable, especially when it starts to get worn so an old-fashioned horn cleat is better in severe conditions. The beauty of the arrangement shown here is that it can be very easily fitted to an existing boom, particularly if there is a track running along the bottom.

Self-tacking jib track

There is an increasing interest in self-tacking headsails which have no booms. These sails need horses which are very carefully designed, otherwise the sail will not set well. The track should be bent to a curve with its radius centred at the point where the forestay touches the deck. The stops at each end of the track are not shown in this sketch and the traveller must be the roller type which slides very easily.

There are various sheeting arrangements possible, but the one in this sketch has the great advantage that only one rope is needed and it can easily be led aft to the cockpit. To make sure that the sail sets really well it is essential to have a plate at the clew with a variety of holes where the block can be shackled, so as to vary the tension on the foot and the leech.

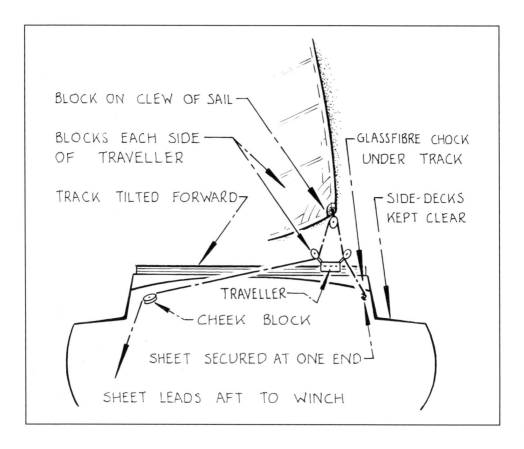

BLOCK ON CLEW OF SAIL

BLOCKS EACH SIDE OF TRAVELLER

GLASSFIBRE CHOCK UNDER TRACK

TRACK TILTED FORWARD

SIDE-DECKS KEPT CLEAR

TRAVELLER

CHEEK BLOCK

SHEET SECURED AT ONE END

SHEET LEADS AFT TO WINCH

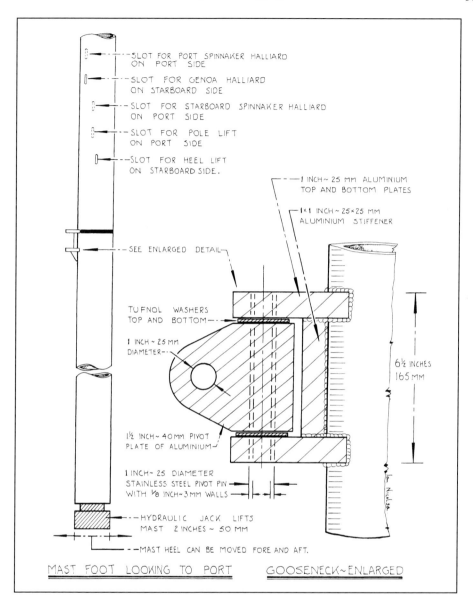

SLOT FOR PORT SPINNAKER HALLIARD
ON PORT SIDE

SLOT FOR GENOA HALLIARD
ON STARBOARD SIDE

SLOT FOR STARBOARD SPINNAKER HALLIARD
ON PORT SIDE

SLOT FOR POLE LIFT
ON PORT SIDE

SLOT FOR HEEL LIFT
ON STARBOARD SIDE.

1 INCH ~ 25 MM ALUMINIUM
TOP AND BOTTOM PLATES

1×1 INCH ~ 25×25 MM
ALUMINIUM STIFFENER

SEE ENLARGED DETAIL

TUFNOL WASHERS
TOP AND BOTTOM

1 INCH ~ 25 MM
DIAMETER

6½ INCHES
165 MM

1½ INCH ~ 40 MM PIVOT
PLATE OF ALUMINIUM

1 INCH ~ 25 DIAMETER
STAINLESS STEEL PIVOT PIN
WITH ⅛ INCH ~ 3 MM WALLS

HYDRAULIC JACK LIFTS
MAST 2 INCHES ~ 50 MM

MAST HEEL CAN BE MOVED FORE AND AFT.

MAST FOOT LOOKING TO PORT   GOOSENECK ~ ENLARGED

Ruthless racing mast

Opponents of the 12-metre *Lionheart* agreed that she had a very sophisticated and effective mast. At its foot it had a hydraulic jack for raising it vertically, and also the heel could be shifted fore and aft. The slots where the halliards came out were carefully staggered so as not to weaken the mast. The gooseneck was extremely simple, compact, easily made and neat.

This drawing should be examined in conjunction with the one showing *Lionheart's* boom overleaf.

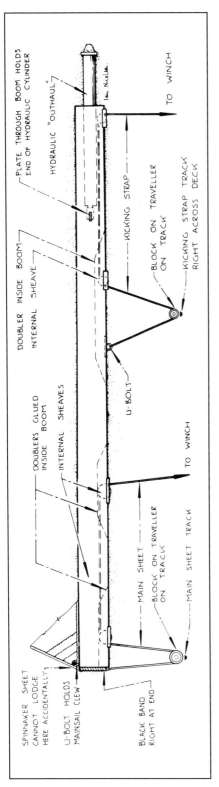

Big boat racing boom

On 12-metre yachts such as *Lionheart*, every effort is made to cut down excess weight and windage. To this end the clew of the mainsail is secured to the extreme outer end of the boom, and to tighten the foot of the mainsail, a hydraulic ram by the gooseneck lengthens the boom as required.

The boom was made light, but stiffened in way of the internal sheaves because each sheave has a slot in the boom which would result in a weakness if there was no local reinforcing.

The main sheet track and the track for the kicking strap were both radiused so that as the boom swung outboard, the main sheet block on the track and the kicking strap block on its track remained in exactly the same position relative to the boom.

This drawing should be studied in conjunction with the one on the previous page showing details of the mast.

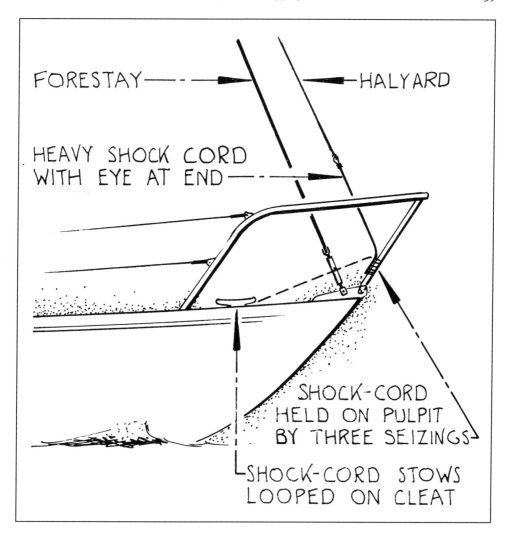

FORESTAY

HALYARD

HEAVY SHOCK CORD
WITH EYE AT END

SHOCK-CORD
HELD ON PULPIT
BY THREE SEIZINGS

SHOCK-CORD STOWS
LOOPED ON CLEAT

Fixing halliard ends

If an unused halliard is secured by strong shock cord it stays tight, out of the way but ready to hand, and should not rattle against the mast. An eye in the top end of the shock cord takes the snap shackle on the end of the halliard.

Instead of shock cord, light line can be used and when not in use holding the halliard it can form a lower rail to the pulpit by being stowed aft around the aft leg of the pulpit, in line with the lower lifeline.

CHAPTER 5

Plumbing

A man is walking along a suburban road, looking for a particular house. He stops at a garden gate and says, 'I'm looking for number 27.'

The fellow in the garden leans on his spade and replies: 'That's Mr Smith's house. It's easy to tell which one because he's a keen boat owner. You can recognise the house, the garden is an unkempt shambles, the window frames all need painting, there are several tiles off the roof and the guttering is overdue for renewing ... but there is a superbly kept boat in the driveway.'

This is a familiar enough story. It's common knowledge that yachtsmen neglect wife and family, house and car, but cherish their boats outrageously. They will spend hours making some inessential gadget for their boat but tolerate a leaking roof and only complain when the bucket used to catch the drips is needed back on the boat.

For my part I find plumbing easy and interesting on boats, but mystifying in houses. Only last month when we had some minor trouble with the lavatory, I tinkered a little and ended up with hot water flushing into the lavatory bowl!

Boat plumbing needs more than ordinary care. Of all the causes of sinking, defective plumbing is absurdly high on the list due to corroded sea-cocks, broken pipes, melted plastic pipes too near to hot exhausts, imperfect pipe joints and so on. There is no doubt that when doing even quite minor plumbing jobs it pays to have a friend, or better still an over-critical rival, look over the finished work for real or potential trouble spots.

Tank gauge (overleaf, top)

Though this tank is shown beneath the cabin sole, its simple gauge can be fitted to a tank located in other positions on board. To see how full the tank is, the watertight screw cap on top is undone and removed, whereupon the vertical brass rod bobs up and the contents of the tank can be read on the marks filed on the rod side. The float must be big enough to support the full weight of the brass rod, but small enough to go right down to the bottom of the tank. The hole for the brass rod should be as small as possible, but of course nowhere near a jamming fit. By having the hole small, there is little risk that fluid will escape through it. The brass rod is screwed into a short threaded socket on top of the float, and there must be an access hole on top of the tank for assembling the float and brass rod inside the tank. When the tank is empty,

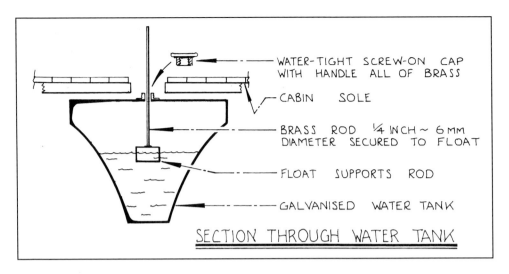

WATER-TIGHT SCREW-ON CAP WITH HANDLE ALL OF BRASS

CABIN SOLE

BRASS ROD ¼ INCH ~ 6 MM DIAMETER SECURED TO FLOAT

FLOAT SUPPORTS ROD

GALVANISED WATER TANK

SECTION THROUGH WATER TANK

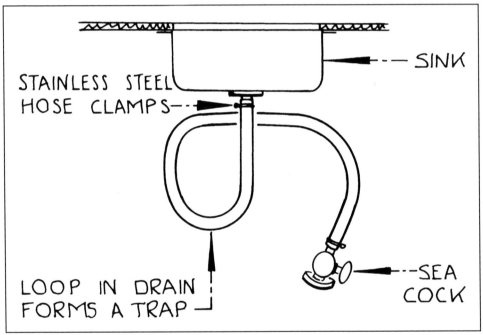

SINK

STAINLESS STEEL HOSE CLAMPS

LOOP IN DRAIN FORMS A TRAP

SEA COCK

the top of the brass rod is just below the watertight screw on the cap. This cap screws onto a short length of tube with a flange which in turn is secured to the tank.

Safe sink drain (above)

It is quite usual to find a drain on a sink which extends steeply down from the bottom of the sink to the seacock, and sometimes the pipe leads overboard without even a seacock. Anything valuable like a wedding ring which is dropped down the sink drain is almost bound to shoot overboard in these circumstances. This annoying possibility is easily eliminated by fitting a longer length of pipe in the form of a loop. There should always be a seacock as well, even on a boat which is used in sheltered waters. Each year quite a few boats sink for want of a simple seacock.

Pumping without bashed knuckles

If a bilge pump is fitted too close to a bulkhead, the crew will find they cannot use the pump properly, and this will be doubly distressing in a crisis. There are two ways round the problem: the handle can be bent or the whole pump can be tilted. The middle sketch shows what may be the quickest way out of the dilemma, with the pump handle either bent or cut and welded. To prevent the pump handle rotating in its socket, the split pin is essential. In some ways, the right hand sketch shows the best approach since this may well make the whole pumping job easier. Before fitting any pump it is best to spend time considering what it will be like working the pump at sea in very rough conditions. The ideal location will be such that the person on the pump can sit in comfort and can use left and right hands alternately to keep going for long periods.

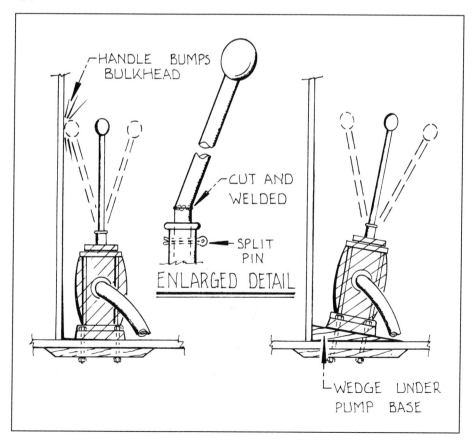

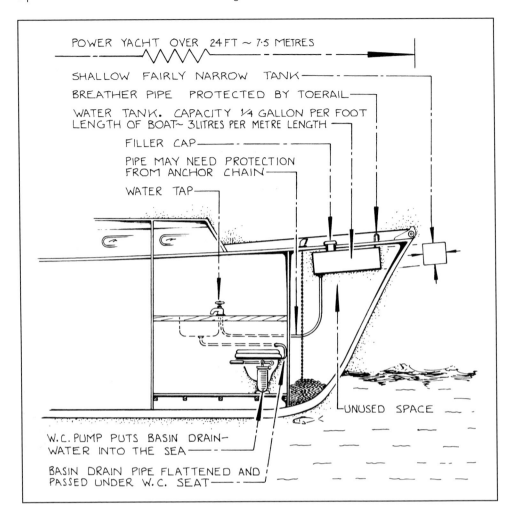

POWER YACHT OVER 24 FT ~ 7·5 METRES

SHALLOW FAIRLY NARROW TANK

BREATHER PIPE PROTECTED BY TOERAIL

WATER TANK. CAPACITY ¼ GALLON PER FOOT
LENGTH OF BOAT~ 3 LITRES PER METRE LENGTH

FILLER CAP

PIPE MAY NEED PROTECTION
FROM ANCHOR CHAIN

WATER TAP

UNUSED SPACE

W.C. PUMP PUTS BASIN DRAIN—
WATER INTO THE SEA

BASIN DRAIN PIPE FLATTENED AND
PASSED UNDER W.C. SEAT

Running water on tap

It is not always easy to have water on tap in a small boat. Usually anyone who wants a drop of water has to pump it up unless, of course, there is a pressure system. But a pressure system is seldom fully reliable, it uses electricity, and many of the pumps are noisy. Provided the boat is big enough, and the quantity of water stored high up is small enough, it is often possible to have a simple gravity feed system. A typical layout will include a tank of modest size, located in an out of the way part of the boat, with its own filler and breather pipe.

The bottom of the tank must be about 18 inches (500 mm) or more above the water tap level and it is almost certainly best to make the system very simple, ideally with only one tap connected to each tank.

The crew have to be warned to turn off the tap, so the type of press down tap which is spring loaded is much the best since it cannot be left on or left dripping.

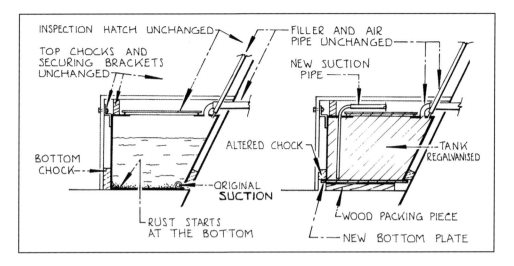

New tank for old (above)

Galvanised steel tanks almost always rust from the bottom upwards. Very often the whole tank is in good condition apart from the bottom plate and the bottom edges of the side plates. Instead of going to the expense of making up a new tank, the old tank can be cut off just above the badly rusted area and a new bottom welded in. The tank is shot blasted and regalvanised, then re-fitted. There will be a small loss of volume and it will be necessary to put packing pieces under the tank to compensate for the lost depth, but the total cost saving can be substantial, since the pipes will all join on to the old tank. However, the old suction may well have been taken off the pipe near the bottom and this might with advantage be changed to a suction which extends up through the top. This reduces the chance of a leak in the tank and also the possibility of dirt getting in the draw-off pipe.

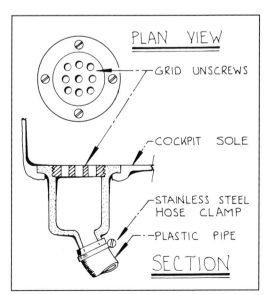

Cockpit drains (left)

Almost all cockpit drains are too small, partly because they have grids on top which limit the rate at which the water can flow down the pipe. What is needed is a small sump to take the grid so that the water can flow through a large grid as fast as it can flow down the drain pipe.

The grid must be designed so that it can be removed for cleaning, and so that the sump can be cleaned out.

A tackable toilet

It is uncomfortable sitting on a WC when a boat is heeled and going to windward. Although a WC cannot be gimballed like a cooker, it can be made to swing through a limited arc (provided it is fixed at a given angle of heel) on either port or starb'd tack.

The whole WC is mounted on a pivoting base with a rigid ratchet secured alongside. A handle engages in the ratchet, so before using the WC all that is necessary to do is to pull the handle out of the ratchet, push the handle across until the top of the WC bowl is level and then release the handle into the nearest notch in the ratchet.

The inlet and outlet pipes have to be flexible and have sufficient spare length to allow the WC to move through the full extent of the ratchet on both tacks.

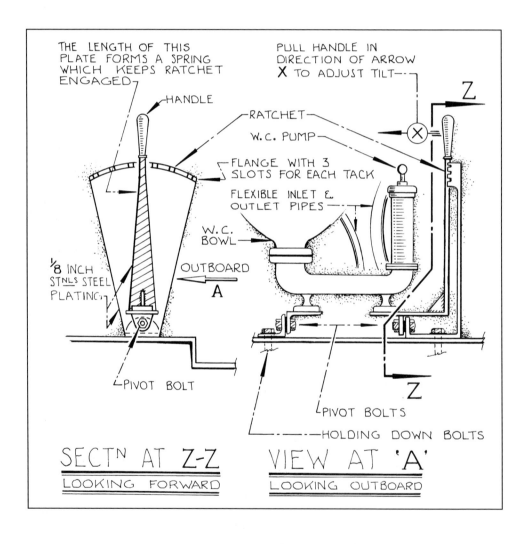

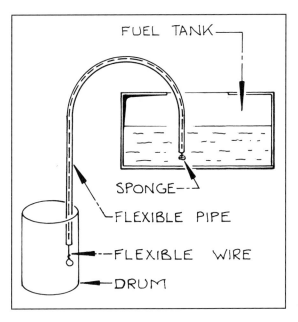

FUEL TANK

SPONGE

FLEXIBLE PIPE

FLEXIBLE WIRE

DRUM

To empty a fuel tank (above left)

The idea of using suction to empty a fuel tank is as old as marine engines. However, nobody likes to put their mouth on the end of a flexible pipe and suck, since they are likely to get a mouthful of fuel if the technique works. To avoid this unpleasant experience, all that is needed is a length of flexible wire and a piece of sponge. One end of the flexible pipe is dipped into the fuel tank and the other extended well below the fuel tank level into a drum. The flexible wire is pulled through the pipe, taking the well secured piece of sponge with it. Fuel is drawn up behind the sponge and the flexible wire pulled right clear of the pipe. As long as the drum is kept well below the level of the fuel tank and the pipe top end is kept well immersed the fuel will run into the drum.

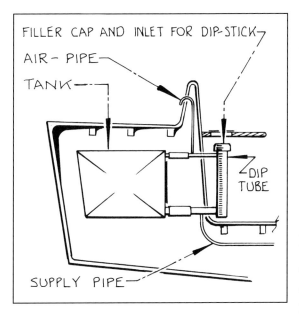

FILLER CAP AND INLET FOR DIP-STICK

AIR - PIPE

TANK

DIP TUBE

SUPPLY PIPE

Inaccessible tank (below left)

There is a simple technique which can be used when a tank has to be fitted in an inaccessible place. The sketch shows how the tank can be put in with all its pipe connections on the only accessible side. There is no need to cut any holes in the deck for the filler, and a dip-stick can be used to find out how much liquid is in the tank.

One disadvantage of this arrangement is that any over-flow or spillage which occurs when filling the tank is likely to run inboard. This can be avoided by having a big drip tray, sometimes called a 'save-all', welded round the filler pipe.

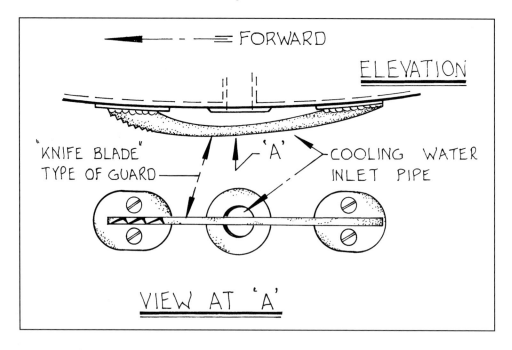

Engine defender

One of the most persistent problems everyone afloat has is the blocking up of engine cooling water intake. The culprit is often a plastic bag which gets itself jammed tightly against the grid over the cooling water intake.

Instead of fitting a normal grid drilled with a number of quite small holes, it can be a much better scheme to have a 'knife blade' guard. This deflects rubbish away from the intake and will cut through some materials. This type of guard is not sold in chandlers and therefore has to be specially made up. It should have at least four through bolts and the serrated cutting edge at the forward end should be kept as sharp as possible.

Better than a dip-stick

A dip-stick has so many disadvantages. For instance, if it is withdrawn when the boat is rolling, the reading will be most inaccurate. Then again, at night or in the rain it can be almost impossible to see just how far up the liquid in the tank has wet the dip-stick.

A more reliable gauge consists of this toughened glass tube with a very small hole at each end. When the tube is withdrawn from the tank, the level of the fluid in the tube shows how much there is in the tank. With a little practice, the crew will soon learn to pull this tube out of the tank and immediately put their finger over the small hole at the bottom to prevent any liquid running out while they make the measurement.

This type of gauge can be used for either fuel or water and it can be inserted in the side as shown or the top of a tank.

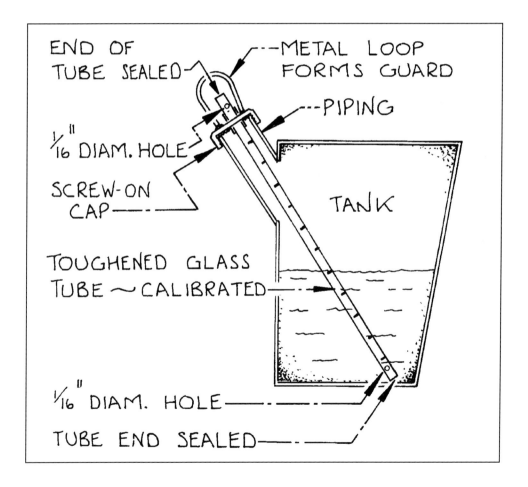

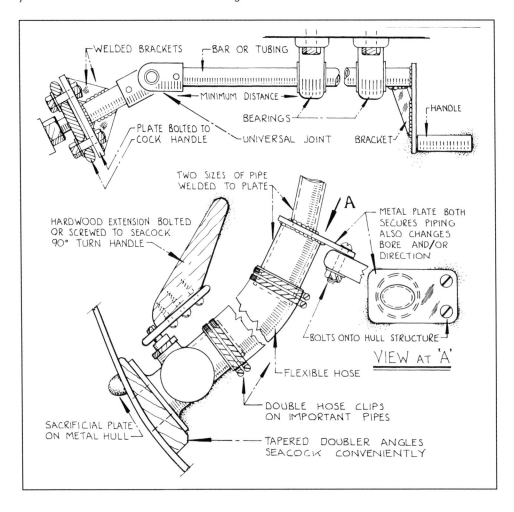

WELDED BRACKETS — BAR OR TUBING

MINIMUM DISTANCE

BEARINGS

PLATE BOLTED TO COCK HANDLE

UNIVERSAL JOINT

HANDLE

BRACKET

TWO SIZES OF PIPE WELDED TO PLATE

HARDWOOD EXTENSION BOLTED OR SCREWED TO SEACOCK 90° TURN HANDLE

METAL PLATE BOTH SECURES PIPING ALSO CHANGES BORE AND/OR DIRECTION

BOLTS ONTO HULL STRUCTURE

VIEW AT 'A'

FLEXIBLE HOSE

SACRIFICIAL PLATE ON METAL HULL

DOUBLE HOSE CLIPS ON IMPORTANT PIPES

TAPERED DOUBLER ANGLES SEACOCK CONVENIENTLY

Plumbing tricks

This sketch shows a variety of tricks which ship's plumbers use. The top sketch shows how an inaccessible seacock can be turned off by remote control. The parts needed can all be bought off the shelf and are simple and fairly cheap. The plate and its extension on the seacock handle will ideally be bolted in place before the deck goes on the ship.

If the handle of the seacock only turns through 90° and is only moderately inaccessible, a simple hardwood extension can sometimes be fitted as shown in the bottom picture. To secure the hardwood to the seacock handle, the handle has to be removed from the seacock and at least three screws should be used to ensure a long lasting permanent bond.

Bottom right, the view at A shows a simple way of changing from one pipe size to another when pipe reducers are not available. A plate is used with a hole drilled in it to suit the smaller pipe, then the smaller pipe is welded on one side lining up with the hole while the larger pipe is welded on the other side of the plate.

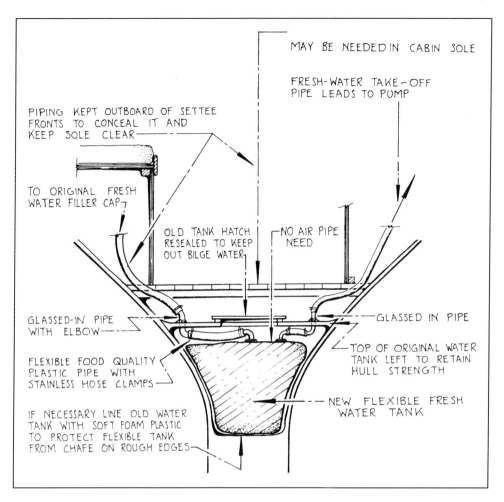

MAY BE NEEDED IN CABIN SOLE

FRESH-WATER TAKE-OFF PIPE LEADS TO PUMP

PIPING KEPT OUTBOARD OF SETTEE FRONTS TO CONCEAL IT AND KEEP SOLE CLEAR

TO ORIGINAL FRESH WATER FILLER CAP

OLD TANK HATCH RESEALED TO KEEP OUT BILGE WATER

NO AIR PIPE NEED

GLASSED-IN PIPE WITH ELBOW

GLASSED IN PIPE

FLEXIBLE FOOD QUALITY PLASTIC PIPE WITH STAINLESS HOSE CLAMPS

TOP OF ORIGINAL WATER TANK LEFT TO RETAIN HULL STRENGTH

IF NECESSARY LINE OLD WATER TANK WITH SOFT FOAM PLASTIC TO PROTECT FLEXIBLE TANK FROM CHAFE ON ROUGH EDGES

NEW FLEXIBLE FRESH WATER TANK

Built-in water tank troubles

Fibreglass boats quite often have built-in fibreglass water tanks. Some of these tanks become dangerous or leaky and osmosis can contaminate the water. This is reported to cause sea-sickness as well as giving the drinking water a foul taste.

It can be difficult, and at times impossible, to repair a built-in water tank, so the alternative is to fit a flexible fresh water tank inside the existing fibreglass one. It is very important to make sure there are no sharp protrusions inside the old tank before the new one is forced in place. As far as possible, the new tank should be about the same size as the space it occupies and if it is smaller it should be chocked off so that it cannot move much when the boat heels or rolls.

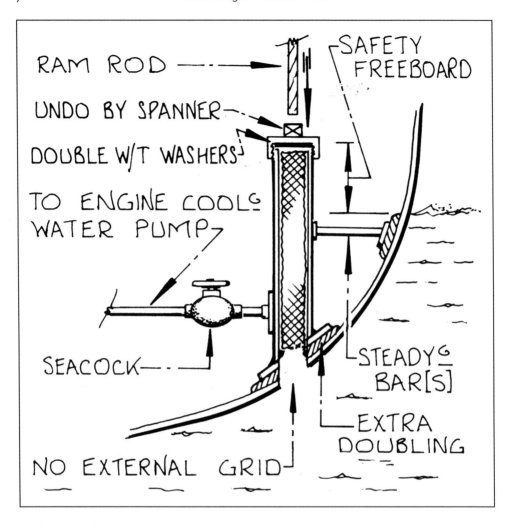

RAM ROD

SAFETY FREEBOARD

UNDO BY SPANNER

DOUBLE W/T WASHERS

TO ENGINE COOLᵍ WATER PUMP

SEACOCK

NO EXTERNAL GRID

STEADYᵍ BAR[S]

EXTRA DOUBLING

Beating polythene bags

Every year, a great number of engines are stopped because the cooling water inlet is blocked by rubbish like polythene bags. Once a bag has jammed itself into the outer end of an intake, it can be extremely difficult to remove without the help of a diver. If the incident happens near the shore, it can cause the ship to be wrecked.

Shown here is an old and well-tried arrangement which allows a crew to clear the cooling water intake while at sea. The main intake need not be exactly vertical, but it must come up in an accessible part of the engine room with plenty of headroom above so that a ramrod can be pushed down the filter to clear obstructions. The filter itself is in the form of a perforated tube or pipe made of wire mesh, loosely fitted inside the main vertical tube which has a flange at the bottom bolted to the hull.

The tube must extend about 18 inches (500 mm) above the waterline as a minimum, so that the cover can be taken off even in a relatively rough sea.

CHAPTER 6

Vents and Hatches

I owned my first cruiser jointly with my sister. We were both young and shared a profound ignorance about many things afloat, so there was a good chance that we would argue a lot, especially when one of our numerous crises developed. We avoided conflict (most of the time) by dividing the boat in half: she stayed aft, I worked forward. She had the helm entering and leaving harbour, during sail changes, getting under way, and so on. I did the fore deck work, grabbed the mooring when we returned home, and reefed ... it was a good division of the trials and triumphs of learning to cruise.

The boat was a converted 6-metre, very long and thin, with no noticeable freeboard, especially offshore. There was no fashion for lifelines, pulpits or personal safety lines in those days and our boat had none of this equipment. Since my sister seldom experienced the delights of changing sails on a submerged fore deck it never occurred to her to slow down. I was too busy and too ignorant to tell her. I thought it was usual to be swept bodily from the forestay into the lee shrouds by deep water sluicing over the deck. Like most beginners, we almost always shortened sail too late and did so while the boat plunged her whole fore-body deep into the wave tops.

There was a forehatch on this boat which had low sleek coamings in keeping with the rest of the boat. As the seas swirled deep over this hatch a lot of water got inboard. More water got in round the mast collar. Water drove in through the main hatch, and more by way of the long open cockpit. Inside the boat it was often as wet as the inside of a shower compartment.

It did seem to us that this was a considerable disadvantage, but it had compensations. One day I started to cook a meal on the primus. The only way to keep the stove stable enough to use was to hold it down on the cabin sole, but I had to let go briefly to open a tin, and the whole cooker tumbled to leeward, spilling burning fuel all over the cabin. It took rather a long time to put out the flames, but the inside of the boat was so saturated that none of the woodwork was charred. The meths just burned on top of the layer of moisture which covered everything. The fire also dried the inside of the boat a little.

Nowadays boats have 'clamp-down' type hatches which should never let in a drop provided they are made strong enough for the job (which means the cheap versions are suspect) and provided they are kept well maintained. However, modern boats are often damp inside because they lack ventilators. Omitting them is one way builders save a little money for themselves ... but in the long run and even in the short term, it is no economy for owners.

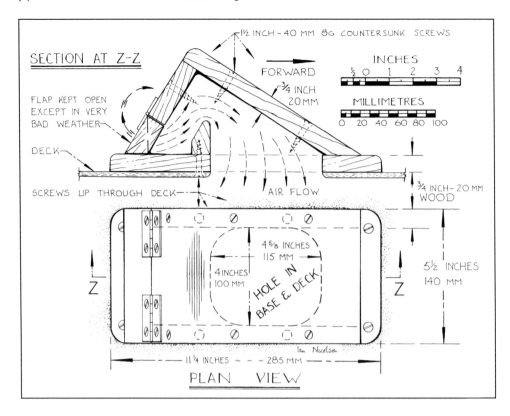

Simple wooden ventilator

This ventilator can easily be made with the minimum tools and material by amateur or professional. It will fit onto a deck or cabin top on a boat made of any material. It can be of hardwood, fibreglass covered softwood, or even plywood. On a bare stark boat, a pair of varnished teak vents like this will improve the whole appearance.

The dimensions will fit a very wide range of craft and can be increased for boats over say, 35 feet (11 metres), but these dimensions should not be reduced except in special circumstances because a smaller ventilator will not give a good flow of air.

The shape is carefully designed to suck in air but to avoid catching ropes, especially headsail sheets. The ventilator will normally have its flap kept open, but in very severe weather, the flap will be dropped down to block off the inlet.

It will normally be necessary to have some sort of clip or barrel bolt to hold the flap open and another to keep it shut. To improve the appearance, the hinges may be recessed and all edges should be well rounded. The two screws or bolts each end are driven downwards and the two screws each side are driven upwards. Ample bedding is put under the base flange, which is extra wide for reliable water-tightness.

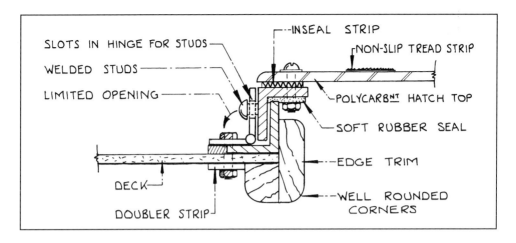

SLOTS IN HINGE FOR STUDS

WELDED STUDS

LIMITED OPENING

INSEAL STRIP

NON-SLIP TREAD STRIP

POLYCARB<u>NT</u> HATCH TOP

SOFT RUBBER SEAL

EDGE TRIM

WELL ROUNDED CORNERS

DECK

DOUBLER STRIP

Homemade forehatch (above)

The modern type of forehatch is such a big advance on the traditional style. The current type has a rubber seal which beds down hard on a metal rim and keeps water out, even if the boat puts her bow completely under a wave. For anyone who cannot afford to buy a standard forehatch, it is not difficult to make one up. All that is needed is some angle bar which is welded up into two square frames, one fitting inside the other. The top one is given a rubber seal all around on the underside of the horizontal flange and perspex (or better super-perspex called polycarbonate) is bolted down on top. The bolts which hold the transparent cover also hold the soft rubber seal. This outside frame is bolted, riveted, or welded to a pair of strong hinges. The inner frame is bolted and well bedded onto the deck or cabin top.

The angle bar can be of seawater resistant aluminium, stainless steel, or a chromium plated brass, but for anybody trying to save money, it will be of galvanised steel. After galvanising, the framework should be degreased and then fully painted, partly to protect the zinc coating and partly to make the hatch look smart. It is important to drill all the holes before the galvanising is carried out.

Foolproof ventilator (overleaf)

This ventilator can stand heavy feet treading on top of it, will not catch sheets, and will let in air but no water unless the weather is really ferocious. Then it is necessary to stop the ventilator up using a wood wedge which is tapped in place as shown in the enlarged section, bottom right. The attraction of this type of ventilator is that it can be made to suit any size of vessel, and from almost any material. It will suit a boat made of fibreglass, wood, or metal and it is easy to fit.

If it is made of galvanised steel, it is best to degrease the fitting and then carefully undercoat and enamel it before fastening it down. This will ensure that the appearance is smart and the galvanising under the paint will last a very long time.

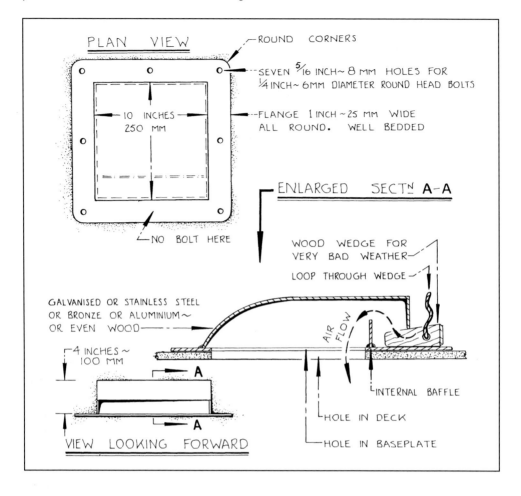

Curing a leaky hatch (opposite)

There is nothing so annoying as a hatch which leaks. Forehatches are worst, because they are most exposed to water coming on board. The most effective cure is to take off the leaking hatch and fit a new, modern type with strong aluminium framework, complete with sharp edge which bites down into the rubber seal when the top is clamped tightly.

Fitting a new hatch can be an expensive way to deal with the problem. A more economical approach is shown here. New baffle pieces are screwed on all four sides of the top, partly to shed water and partly to make it more difficult for water to drive in. Close by these baffle pieces on each side, there is a new rim piece which also acts as a baffle to water running along the deck. Before the boat goes to sea, a tight PVC waterproof cover is fitted over the top, its bottom edge being pulled taut by the line which runs through the seam all round. If a long voyage is being undertaken, a second waterproof cover is worth fitting and, as the hatch is to be secured semi-permanently, it can also be sealed with Sylglass tape or a similar non-hardening compound.

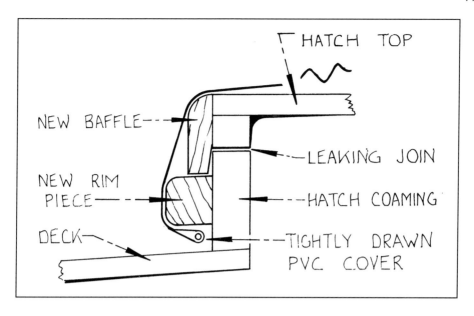

Clam shell ventilator (below)

This moulded fibreglass ventilator was designed by McGruers for a 65-foot (20-metre) powerboat. One of these ventilators was fitted on each side of the wheelhouse. One feature of this design is that a single mould fits either port or starboard sides since the inlet hole at the bottom is cut after the whole ventilator has been moulded. Anyone wanting to make a ventilator like this can increase or decrease the dimensions. However, it is important to note that the inlet at the bottom is larger than the hole cut at the wheelhouse side which, in turn, is larger than the fan inlet duct.

In short, when designing a ventilator, the size of each aperture should be progressively smaller in the direction of the airflow.

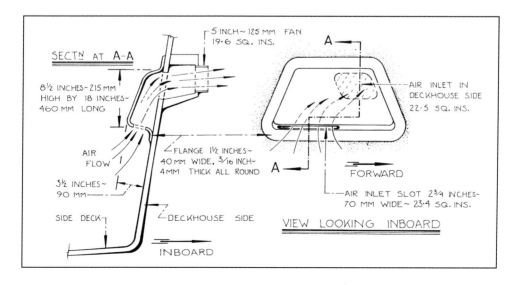

Instead of weatherboards

The ordinary weatherboards which drop into a hatch-way have several disadvantages. They block light, they seldom have ventilators, and they can be inconvenient to lift in and out if they are big or heavy.

At the beginning of a cruise, it can be very pleasant to put the weatherboards away, at least until bad weather sets in, and have this simple flexible screen instead. If the screen is made of a translucent material, it will let lots of light into the cabin and the slits at either side will give some ventilation.

In hot weather, the flexible screen will keep out the sun and in wet weather, the rain will be deflected away. The screen should be made wider than the opening at the bottom and it will need a heavy batten stitched into the lower seam to prevent the wind blowing the screen sideways. When not in use, the screen is rolled up and secured by tapes on top of the sliding hatch. In very bad weather, the screen can be dropped down to form an extra water barrier to help the weatherboards keep out heavy seas.

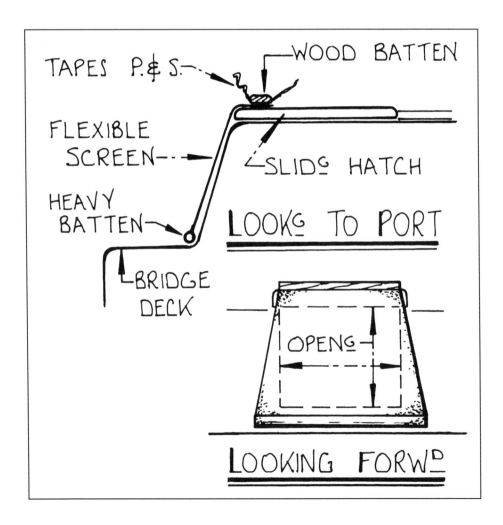

CHAPTER 7

Deck Fittings

When my father was an apprentice, the firm he worked for built three identical tugs. For some reason (which has been lost in the many years since these events) someone in authority decided to test all three tugs to the limit. The first tug was secured to a strong point ashore by a long, strong, towing hawser of the thickest and most unbreakable wire. She was pointed away from the shore and accelerated off at her best speed. The towing wire came taut with an extremely severe jolt, and the towing hook broke.

The second tug was lined up and put through the same test, and this time the towing hook carriage sheered. When the third tug was put to it, her deck tore off in way of the towing hook carriage.

'And that,' my father used to say when he told me about these trials, 'proved just how good our design work was. All the components were just about the same strength, so a different one failed each time. If it had always been the same one which broke we would have seen that it was too weak.'

This was all very instructive for a youngster, and it makes a keen draughtsman strive to get everything designed with precisely the right strength yet with not an ounce of wasted material or labour. But hold on a minute. Is it a good idea to have the deck tearing off? I rather think not. If a fitting fails at sea, that is bad and may be disastrous. However, if a fitting holds on to the deck, but the deck is wrenched off leaving a vast hole, that is usually worse. Fittings break mainly in bad weather and that is no time to have large pieces of decking disappear over the side.

No one is advocating components with built-in weaknesses, but a very good case can be made for having base flanges stronger than the upper part of any fitting. And if a fitting does fail, it is a happy crew which has a substitute nearby to serve till repairs are made. That is why well-finished ocean cruisers always have an extra cleat each side near the cockpit, and a pair of spare cleats on the mast ... and so on.

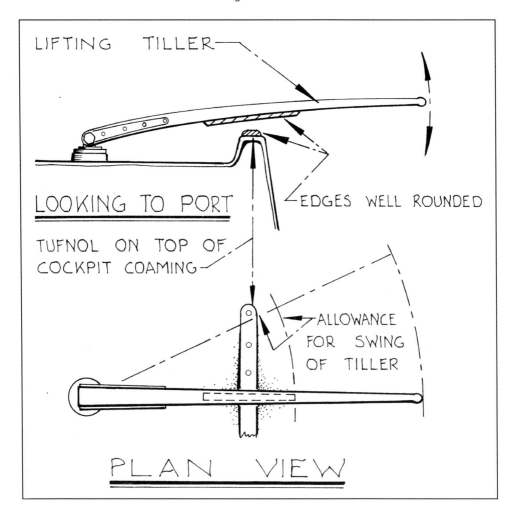

LIFTING TILLER

LOOKING TO PORT

EDGES WELL ROUNDED

TUFNOL ON TOP OF
COCKPIT COAMING

ALLOWANCE
FOR SWING
OF TILLER

PLAN VIEW

Protecting tiller and cockpit coaming

When a tiller is hinged at the rudder stock head there is always a risk of chafe to both the cockpit coaming and the tiller where the two touch. It is best to prevent this damage by fixing a length of tufnol or similar semi-hard plastic to the underside of the tiller and another piece to the top of the cockpit coaming.

The piece on the tiller will be held by screws countersunk so that their heads are about $\frac{1}{16}$ inch (1.5 mm) below the top surface of the tufnol. The screws will be spaced approximately 2 inches (50 mm) apart.

The tufnol on the top of the coaming will have screws or bolts countersunk the same distance and here the fastenings can be spread out about 4 inches (100mm) because the material is being loaded along its length. In each case the plastic will probably be something like 1 ½ inches × ¼ inch (30 mm × 6 mm) in section.

Stowing a life ring

These four methods of storing a life ring are designed for use on a flat deck, but apart from the one at the bottom left, they can be used on a vertical surface.

The top two stowage techniques involve the use of Terylene bags, and these can be obtained from a local sail-maker. He should be given the life ring so that he can make the bags to fit exactly. Some people will favour tanned Terylene because it does not show the dirt, and others will prefer a PVC waterproof material. This material can be obtained in a bright orange colour which will certainly make the life ring easy to see.

The open topped box shown at the bottom on the right has many advantages, but the shock cord will need renewing every two or three years since it tends to perish when exposed to sunlight. Whatever technique is used, the life ring should be placed so that it can be quickly reached by the helmsman. The arrangement shown top left, for instance, should be secured on deck so that the grab line which is just outside the Terylene bag is within reach of the helmsman's grasp.

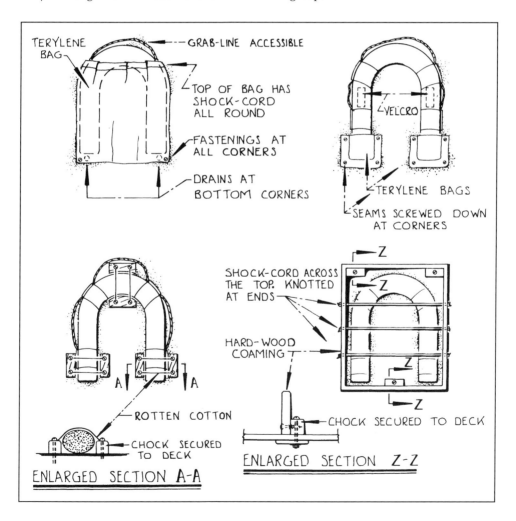

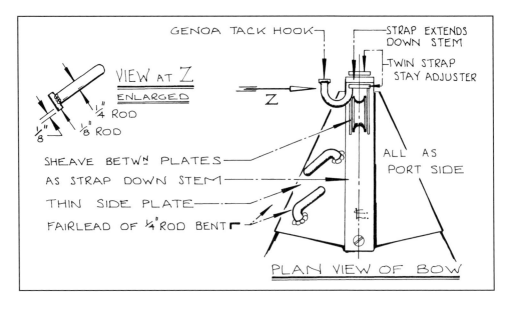

Small boat stemhead

This fitting is suitable for boats of around 27 feet (8 metres) and less. It is intended for boats which lie in marinas, which explains why there is no stemhead roller for a permanent mooring. To make the whole fitting light, it is fabricated from thin plate turned down over the topsides and secured port and starb'd. Welded to this is a thicker strap on top of the deck plate, with a similar strap welded to the forward end extending down the forward side of the stem with fastenings through the stem. This forward strap extends upwards and has a hole in it to take the twin strap stay adjuster which is used instead of a rigging screw.

The 'pig's tail' hooks port and starb'd for taking the head sail tack are a slightly unusual design with a T-bar end to prevent the tack coming unhooked. A sheave is worked between two upstanding plates to take the headsail Cunningham line. This sheave is not satisfactory for the spinnaker boom downhaul because when the boom swings outboard the downhaul rope would chafe badly. And those bent rods forming the fairleads port and starb'd are only satisfactory in well sheltered harbours; they probably would not stand up to very severe conditions.

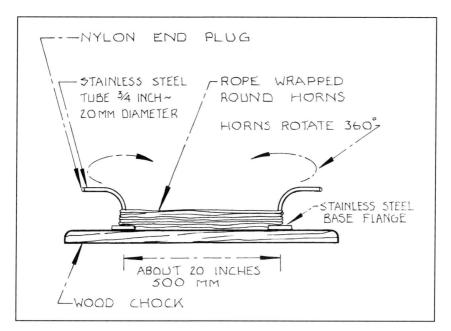

NYLON END PLUG

STAINLESS STEEL
TUBE ¾ INCH ~
20 MM DIAMETER

ROPE WRAPPED
ROUND HORNS

HORNS ROTATE 360°

STAINLESS STEEL
BASE FLANGE

ABOUT 20 INCHES
500 MM

WOOD CHOCK

Warp stowage (above)

If a rope is stowed hung up against the inside of a boat, it may chafe and become seriously worn as the boat rolls or pitches. A rope thrown carelessly into the bottom of a locker is not quickly available in an emergency. Ideally, everything on a boat should be so convenient that it can be grabbed and used without a second's thought.

If a rope is wrapped around two horns, and not pulled too tight, it will be kept well aired and dry out easily. When the rope is needed the horns are swung in towards each other and the rope is quickly lifted off. In practice it is only necessary to swing one horn round and the rope is lifted off at that end.

The attraction of this idea is that it can be used on all sizes of boat. The wood chock base can be bolted down, or fixed in a temporary way. The chock might be on the fore deck, down inside an anchor locker, secured permanently or occasionally on the aft deck, or fitted on the underside of a locker lid; the alternatives are numerous.

Moveable personal lifelines (overleaf, top)

One of the main disadvantages of personal lifelines (which each crew member should have secured to his body in bad weather) is that they limit freedom of movement.

However, this can be overcome in an economical way if the lifeline is clipped onto a carriage on the genoa sheet lead track. Some of these tracks extend over a considerable length of the boat, but even if they are only a few feet long this is much better than a fixed securing point. It may be necessary to fit one or two extra carriages to each track, on each side. Naturally, the track and carriages must be

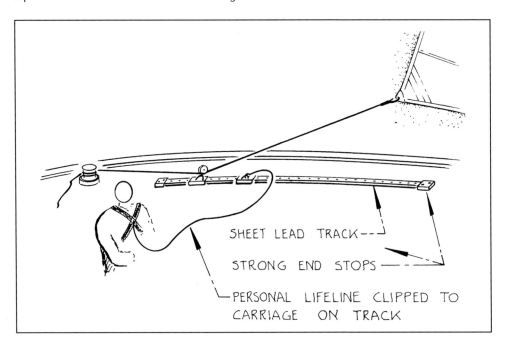

SHEET LEAD TRACK---┘

STRONG END STOPS ———

└PERSONAL LIFELINE CLIPPED TO
CARRIAGE ON TRACK

substantial, as they are on most boats over 30 feet (9 metres) long. However, smaller boats sometimes have flimsy tracks and carriages and these should be replaced since even the genoa sheet may cause breakages in severe weather. Whatever track is used, it should have very stout end stops, each secured with at least two bolts right through deck and an underdeck doubler pad.

Anchor chock and lashing

This is one of the cheapest and simplest ways of holding an anchor down on deck. An eyebolt complete with wood pad is secured down to the deck, and a shackle made fast through it. The size of the shackle is selected so that it fits neatly round the anchor. If the shackle is a little too large, it can have a whipping of light line round it so that the hole where the anchor shank goes is reduced in size.

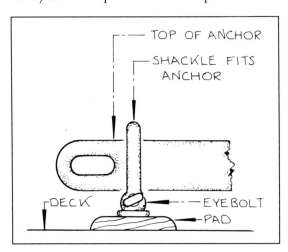

TOP OF ANCHOR

SHACKLE FITS
ANCHOR

DECK

EYEBOLT

PAD

Though the top of the anchor is shown through the shackle, eyebolts and shackles can be used on stocks, on Danforth cross-bars and so on.

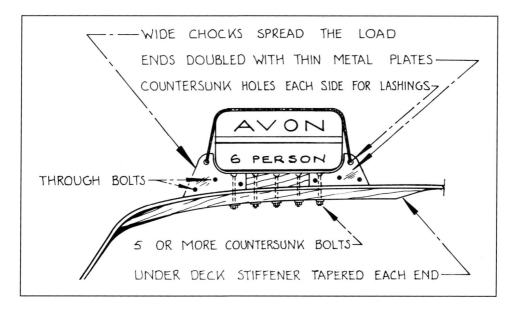

WIDE CHOCKS SPREAD THE LOAD

ENDS DOUBLED WITH THIN METAL PLATES

COUNTERSUNK HOLES EACH SIDE FOR LASHINGS

AVON

6 PERSON

THROUGH BOLTS

5 OR MORE COUNTERSUNK BOLTS

UNDER DECK STIFFENER TAPERED EACH END

Chocks for life raft (above)

In very severe conditions (for instance when a boat is rolled right over) there have been occasions when a life raft stowed on deck has been swept overboard. It is not enough to secure a life raft with two or even four small eyebolts. Even eyeplates can be inadequate if they are too small or are held by under-sized bolts through a flimsy deck.

A good arrangement is to have a pair of wide chocks forming a strong cradle. If the chocks are made of hardwood and curved up at each end, there will be short grain where the side lips turn up to prevent the life raft from sliding off. To strengthen these upstanding ends thin metal plates on one, or better still both, sides of each chock are bolted through at each end. Holes drilled right through will take the two lashings on the life raft and, of course, these lashings must have quick release arrangements. To be safe, there should be two ways of releasing the lashing, such as a heavy duty snap shackle and a rope lashing which can be cut.

Anchor winch modification (overleaf, top)

Anchor winches, being on the fore deck, suffer a great deal from the weather. Every time a boat puts her bow under a wave the winch gets soused. It is inevitable that anchor winches need more maintenance than other fittings, particularly as they have to carry heavy loads.

When it comes to dismantling a winch, the work can be very difficult indeed, especially if the keys holding the barrels onto the axles are seized. A modification which can be made involves leaving all the keys out and fitting a tapped-in bolt instead. The keyway is drilled out to a round hole and this is then tapped to take a suitable size of bolt, and, incidentally, a size which is easy to obtain.

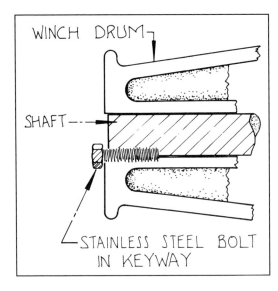

WINCH DRUM

SHAFT

STAINLESS STEEL BOLT
IN KEYWAY

Strong point (bottom left)

For so many jobs an eyeplate bolted through a deck is the best fitting. Eyeplates in different sizes made of stainless steel or bronze are easy to obtain from chandlers. They are cheap and easy to make from mild steel extrusions or welded up from mild steel plate. If mild steel is used, all the edges should be carefully ground round and then the fitting should be hot-dip galvanised. Before bolting it down to preserve the galvanising it is best to degrease the fitting and then build up three coats of paint.

The best eyeplates have four bolts in all, though for a very light deck and a heavily loaded fitting it might pay to have a bigger base flange and eight or more bolts all well spread out.

The fairing pieces in front and behind are a nice detail, and particularly valuable if the eyeplate is located where it is likely to catch genoa or spinnaker sheets.

It is rare to see *double* underdeck doublers but certainly for deep sea work this is the best arrangement. All the doublers should have bevelled edges not just to avoid hard spots, but also to help paint or varnish stay on.

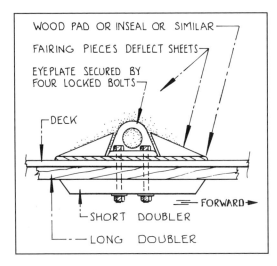

WOOD PAD OR INSEAL OR SIMILAR

FAIRING PIECES DEFLECT SHEETS

EYEPLATE SECURED BY
FOUR LOCKED BOLTS

DECK

FORWARD

SHORT DOUBLER

LONG DOUBLER

Stemhead fitting for sailing yacht (opposite)

This fitting was designed for a cruiser racer 30 feet (9 metres) overall. However, it would suit a great variety of boats between about 25 and 36 feet (7.5 and 11 metres).

The thimble holding plate is an ingenious way of securing the tack of the headsail, but it is essential that each headsail has the same size of tack eye. Also the thimble holding plates (since there is one on each side of the stemhead fitting), must be made so that they just fit neatly through the tack eye. Yet another important consideration is that the crew must be familiar with this type

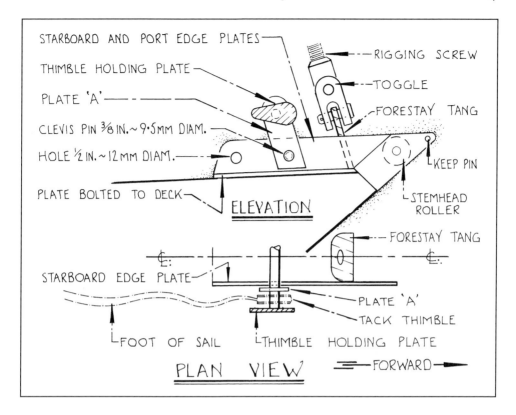

STARBOARD AND PORT EDGE PLATES

THIMBLE HOLDING PLATE

PLATE 'A'

CLEVIS PIN ⅜ IN. ~ 9·5MM DIAM.

HOLE ½ IN. ~ 12MM DIAM.

PLATE BOLTED TO DECK

RIGGING SCREW

TOGGLE

FORESTAY TANG

KEEP PIN

STEMHEAD ROLLER

ELEVATION

FORESTAY TANG

STARBOARD EDGE PLATE

FOOT OF SAIL

THIMBLE HOLDING PLATE

PLATE 'A'

TACK THIMBLE

PLAN VIEW

FORWARD

of fitting, otherwise they will have trouble at night when changing headsails in a hurry.

The whole fitting is low and sleek and should not be heavy, but it shows two important mistakes, quite often found on modern boats where style is rated higher than reliability. First of all, the anchor chain or mooring warp cannot conveniently come in over the roller and straight off because the forestay tang is in the way. Secondly, the keep-pin is much too low and if the boat ranges about on the moorings, the keep-pin is likely to be over-stressed and eventually fail. The mooring chain will then ride out over the side ears of the stemhead roller and cause a lot of damage to the boat's deck edge and even the hull.

Layout of deck fittings (overleaf)

The *Contention 33* (10 metres or 33 feet overall) has a good layout for frequent racing and occasional cruising.

The main winches are well inboard where the crew can work in relative comfort. The sheets come from the roller fairleads on the genoa sheet lead track, by way of the Lewmar 9413 sheaves flat on deck and then inboard to the main winches. By the companionway there are winches for reefing, adjusting the Cunningham hole on the luff of the mainsail and so on.

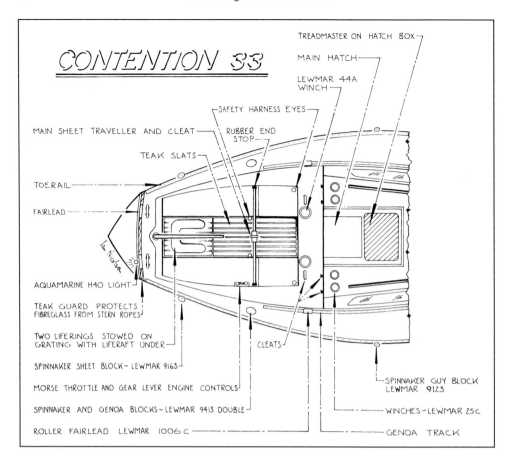

This drawing should be viewed in conjunction with the one which shows the layout from amidships forward.

Layout of deck gear on *Contention 33* (opposite)

The drawing opposite should be studied in conjunction with the one above. It shows the forward end of the boat, with spinnaker poles stowed close up against the toerails port and starb'd, leaving a relatively clear fore deck and side decks.

The halliard winches are located aft of the mast. When the headsail halliards are not in use, their forward ends are clipped onto the special rail fitted on the mast step base plate. This is shown in an enlarged detail, top right.

Not shown in either sketch are the stanchions and aft pulpit, but of course there are upper and lower lifelines right round the boat.

This layout is intended for a full crew. If the boat was to be used for cruising with only a limited number of people on board, the layout would be modified quite a bit.

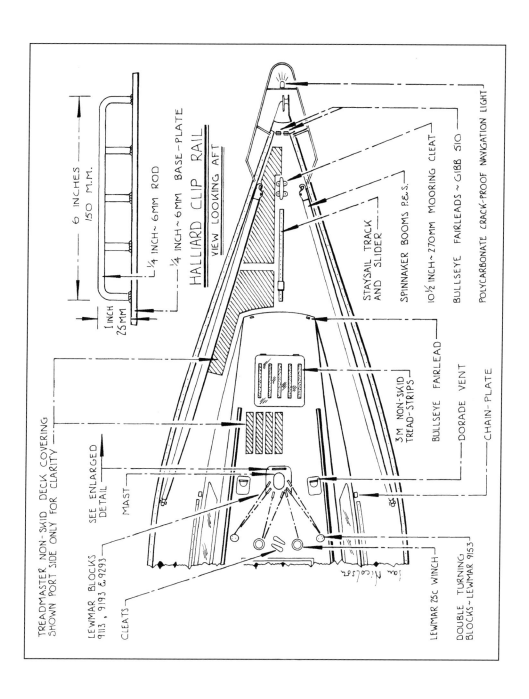

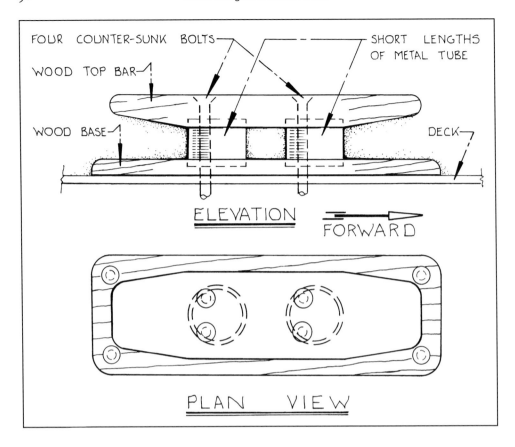

FOUR COUNTER-SUNK BOLTS

SHORT LENGTHS
OF METAL TUBE

WOOD TOP BAR

WOOD BASE

DECK

ELEVATION

FORWARD

PLAN   VIEW

Mooring cleat

The cheapest way to make a mooring cleat is either to build it up from pieces of wood glued together, or use a solid chock. However, the mooring wire or chain is likely to chafe the wood and in time may make the whole cleat dangerously weak. The cleat shown here is assembled from a base plank and top wood bar (both of which are smallish and therefore cheap pieces of wood), with metal tube legs. The metal tubes can be of stainless steel or bronze: aluminium is likely to chafe and galvanised steel will soon rust.

The tubes are slightly recessed into the base and the top bar. The exposed length of tube should be about twice the diameter of the mooring wire, or twice the width of the mooring chain links.

The bolts which hold the whole fitting down also clamp the upper wood bar, the tubes and the base altogether. Because the pull of the mooring is forward, the vertical bolts are tight up against the tubes at their aft sides.

The length of the cleat will depend not only on the size of the boat but the amount of shelter there is where she is moored. Typically the cleat would be about $\frac{1}{27}$ of the length of the boat.

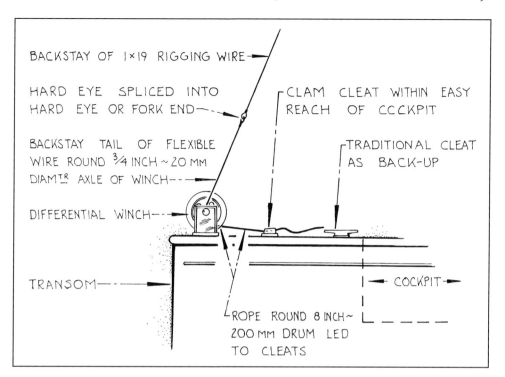

BACKSTAY OF 1×19 RIGGING WIRE→

HARD EYE SPLICED INTO
HARD EYE OR FORK END—··

BACKSTAY TAIL OF FLEXIBLE
WIRE ROUND ¾ INCH ~20 MM
DIAMᵀᴿ AXLE OF WINCH—·—

DIFFERENTIAL WINCH—·

TRANSOM—··—

┌CLAM CLEAT WITHIN EASY
│ REACH OF COCKPIT

┌TRADITIONAL CLEAT
│ AS BACK-UP

|◄— COCKPIT —►

└ROPE ROUND 8 INCH~
200 MM DRUM LED
TO CLEATS

Backstay tensioner

This arrangement was used on a Quarter Tonner, and has the great virtue of simplicity and speed of operation. Differential winches are normally used for lifting centreboards in dinghies, and as a result they are available through yacht chandlers. A typical power ratio is about 10 or 12 to 1.

As the wire and rope are permanently on the winch, no time is wasted in tightening or slackening the backstay. A clam cleat is normally used to hold the rope which comes forward off the winch, but it may be found that this type of cleat needs a back-up, perhaps because the cleat is slightly worn or possibly because one of the crew may accidentally kick the rope out of the cleat. So in practice the crew may first jam the rope in the clam cleat, and when they have more time they secure it round the traditional horned cleat for extra safety.

Where the rope comes off the differential winch, a 2 to 1 purchase can be introduced if the winch itself does not give quite enough power. This 2 to 1 purchase can be in the form of a single block on the end of the rope which comes off the winch and another rope led through the block with each end extending to the side decks, port and starb'd. This allows the crew sitting out on the side deck to adjust the backstay without moving.

Fairlead lock

When a boat is tied up alongside a quay wall which is higher than the deck edge, the mooring warps are likely to be pulled out of the fairleads. This can be particularly dangerous in rough conditions if the boat is plunging about. To keep a rope, or indeed two or three ropes, safely inside a fairlead all that is needed is a piece of bent plate and two bolts or drop-nose pins. The plate is made long enough so that even though it can slide fore and aft slightly it can never get off the fairlead until one of the bolts is released. Naturally, the bolts must have one of the various types of nuts which will not come off accidentally.

Though this fitting is shown on a fairlead made from a round bar welded into a metal toerail, the principle can be applied to many types of fairlead.

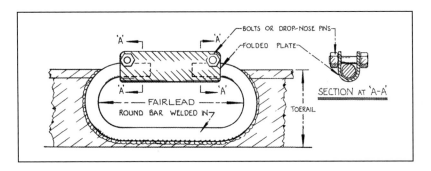

Sheet or halliard stowage box

This idea was originally seen on a yacht called *Galway Blazer*. She had a high flush deck, with a heavily rounded camber. On a boat like this, ropes tend to fall overboard all too easily. Also she was sailed short-handed so it was particularly important that ropes were kept under control.

Though the sheet boxes were made of fibreglass, they could be made of polythene, wood or metal. If they are let into a deck, it is essential that the deck is properly strengthened to compensate for the hole which has been cut out. There must be plenty of bedding all-round the rim to keep out the water.

If the sheet or halliard box is made of a transparent material, it will act as a deadlight and let daylight into the hull. Care will be needed that the drainage does not get bunged up with dirt since it is only ½ inch (12 mm) and this size has, in the past, suffered from blocking by the usual rubbish which finds its way on board as, for instance, when a boat is tied up alongside a quay.

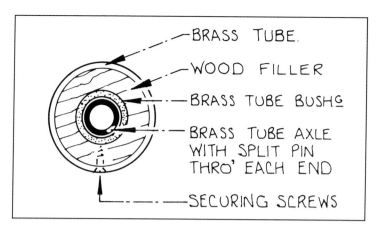

- BRASS TUBE.
- WOOD FILLER
- BRASS TUBE BUSH<u>G</u>
- BRASS TUBE AXLE WITH SPLIT PIN THRO' EACH END
- SECURING SCREWS

Homemade stemhead roller

A stemhead roller made of any plastic material never lasts long. Chain or wire quickly chafes it away and it gradually becomes more and more useless.

Anyone who does not have a lathe may find it difficult to make up his own stemhead roller. However, it is not too difficult to buy brass or bronze tubes of different diameters. Using a selection of different sized tubes and wood filler pieces, an amateur can make up a reasonably long lasting stemhead roller which will stand up to several years hard usage. If the boat in question lies on an open anchorage, it may be good practice to make up several rollers at the same time so that there is a stock of spares.

Instead of using a wood filler, fibreglass cloth and resin might be used instead.

Securing headsail tacks

One or two strong hooks are sometimes fixed to the stemhead plate of a sailing yacht to take the tack eyes of headsails. Once the sail has been hoisted up tight there is no chance that the eye will fall off the hook, but during the hoisting process this annoying accident may happen.

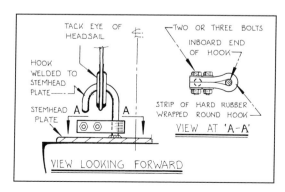

TACK EYE OF HEADSAIL

TWO OR THREE BOLTS

INBOARD END OF HOOK

HOOK WELDED TO STEMHEAD PLATE

STRIP OF HARD RUBBER WRAPPED ROUND HOOK

STEMHEAD PLATE

A

A

VIEW AT 'A-A'

VIEW LOOKING FORWARD

To lock the eye onto the hook all that is needed is a strip of hard rubber wrapped around the hook and secured with two bolts so that there is plenty of friction between the rubber and the vertical leg of the hook. The rubber is swung forward or aft until the sail has been slipped onto the hook, then the rubber is swung outboard to prevent the tack eye falling off the hook.

Pulpit to suit spinnaker chute

On those small decked boats which have spinnaker chutes, it is important to have the kind of pulpit which makes spinnaker hoisting easy. There must be no sharp angles between any two bars of the pulpit where the sail might jam on its way up or down.

The pulpit sketched here is designed for double chutes so that, for instance, the crew have a choice of hoisting a star cut from one side and maximum area spinnaker from the other.

Since a chute on a yacht is often associated with a sunken self-draining cockpit forward, the inset drawing top left is of special interest. It shows one way of getting this cockpit quickly freed of accumulated spray or water.

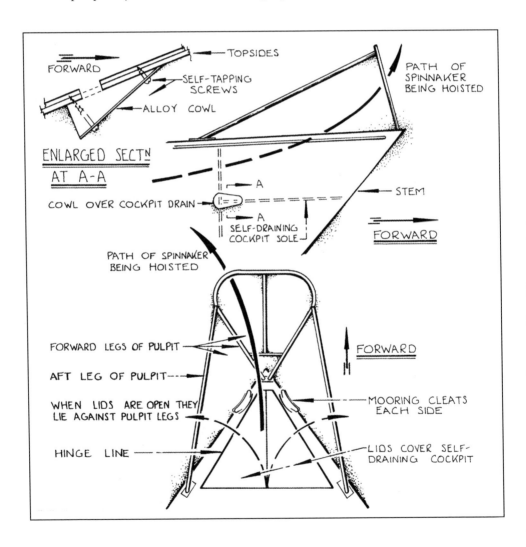

Teak bar cleat

The old-fashioned and much admired teak bar cleat was made up of bronze cast ends which were bolted to the deck. This type of cleat is no longer available, so a new design has been dreamed up to suit modern production methods. The base plate is wide and long so as to spread the load over a good area of deck. It has a bolt at each corner and either two or four more. Two bolts are welded at their heads onto the baseplate and tubes slipped over these bolts. Next, the teak bar is slid onto the up-ended bolts, then washers and cap nuts added.

To revarnish the teak bar, the cap nuts are removed and the bar taken off. This must be done each winter and one of the special features of this design is that even if the bar is heavily sandpapered or lightly planed, it will still fit back on the base.

The base plate, tubes and bolts must all be of the same material, which may be seawater resistant stainless steel or bronze, but not common brass or galvanised mild steel.

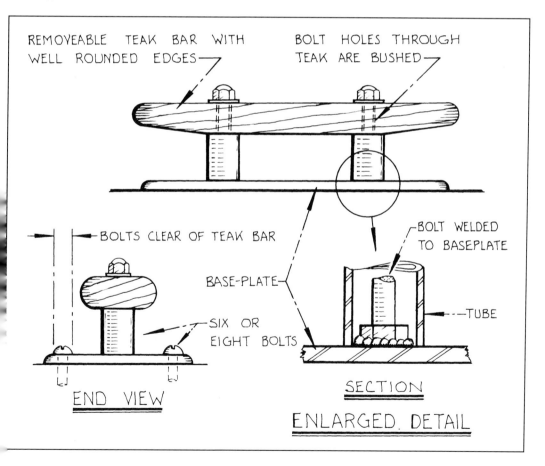

REMOVEABLE TEAK BAR WITH WELL ROUNDED EDGES

BOLT HOLES THROUGH TEAK ARE BUSHED

BOLTS CLEAR OF TEAK BAR

BASE-PLATE

SIX OR EIGHT BOLTS

BOLT WELDED TO BASEPLATE

TUBE

END VIEW

SECTION

ENLARGED. DETAIL

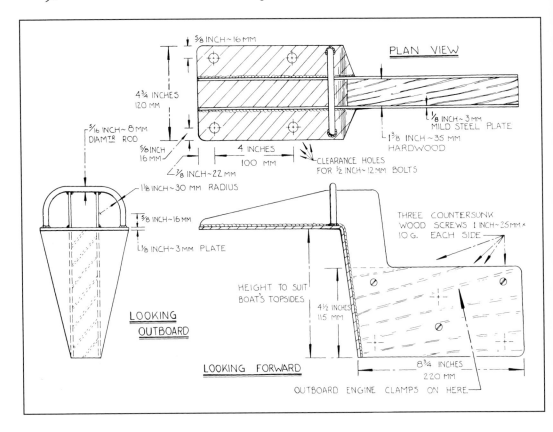

Side fitting outboard bracket

If a day racing boat or a small cruiser uses an outboard engine to get home in calm weather, it is very often much better to fit the engine abreast of the cockpit rather than on the stern. A special bracket is needed but normally this is a relatively simple portable unit.

The one shown here was designed by McGruer's for a Piper Class yacht and is typical of good engineering practice. It will fit a variety of boats and engines up to about 8 horse power.

There should be a wooden pad on deck to take the horizontal plate of the bracket and another wooden pad under the deck. These pads should ideally be twice as big as the steel plate and each about ½ inch (12 mm) thick. The ½-inch bolts which hold the bracket are tightened by butterfly nuts.

The safety line tied to the engine can be made fast to the ⁵⁄₁₆-inch (8-mm) rod which forms the fore and aft stiffener for the vertical plates. The whole fitting is galvanised before the wood chock is put in place, and after all the metal edges have been ground to a good radius. The fitting could be made of stainless steel or a non-ferrous metal but mild steel galvanised tends to be the cheapest. All the plating in the drawing is ⅛ inch (3 mm) and anybody who is weight conscious could cut some lightening holes in all the plates.

Locking in headsail tacks

Here is another variant where tacks are secured to a single stainless steel hook, or more often a pair of hooks, located at the foot of the forestay. When a headsail is being hoisted, the tack eye is slipped onto the hook. It should stay there until the sail is tight up when there is no risk that the sail can fall off the hook, but it often falls off while the sail goes up. To prevent this infuriating habit, one method is to screw a piece of soft plastic in a loop beneath the eye. This plastic can be obtained by cutting a strip out of a plastic food box or plastic bowl.

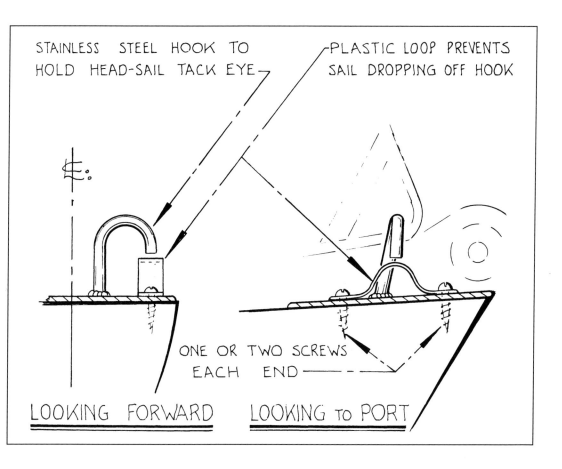

STAINLESS STEEL HOOK TO HOLD HEAD-SAIL TACK EYE

PLASTIC LOOP PREVENTS SAIL DROPPING OFF HOOK

ONE OR TWO SCREWS EACH END

LOOKING FORWARD   LOOKING TO PORT

Improving a bar cleat

Nothing looks so attractive on the deck of any boat as a bar cleat. Such a gleaming varnished teak bar through polished bronze or stainless legs raises the standard of appearance of every type of craft.

However, the teak bar has to be taken out for revarnishing each year and this may involve unbolting the whole cleat. Many of these cleats have screws driven upwards through the tubular section of the leg to retain the teak bar. It is almost impossible, even with a small screwdriver with its shank bent at right angles, to remove these hidden screws. For this reason, some skippers have a new set of screws fitted which are driven vertically downwards from the top.

These screws have to be taken out each year since the teak bar should never be rubbed down and revarnished in place, but removed from its metal legs so that a proper job can be done. This means the screws should be put in well-greased.

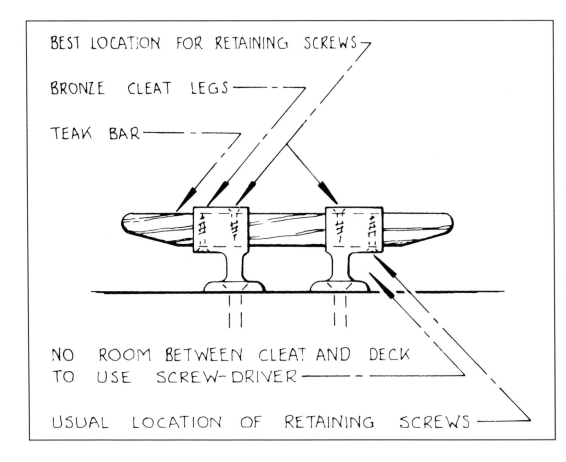

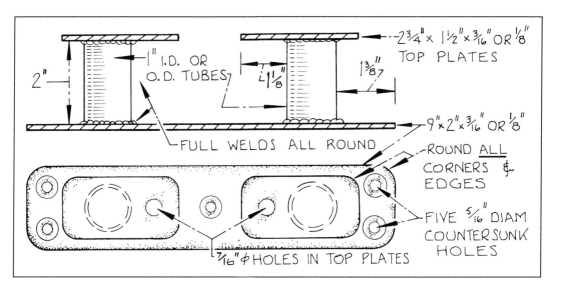

Combined fairlead and bollards (above)

Anybody who makes up his own fittings will find this one very easy. It is a fairlead made from flat plate and metal piping and it can be fabricated from stainless steel, bronze, or mild steel which is later galvanised.

It could even be made from aluminium, though this must be seawater resistant and will not stand up to the chafe of wire or chain.

Whatever metal is used, all the edges and corners must be ground away carefully. All the welding must be to a good standard and continuous all round.

This fitting can be scaled up or even slightly reduced, but the gap between the top plates must be at least 1 ¾ times the diameter of the largest rope likely to be placed in the fairlead or round the horns, when it is used as a bollard. The top plates can be joined by a lashing if the boat is lying alongside, with her deck below quay wall height. Without a lashing, some ropes will tend to lift out of the fairlead.

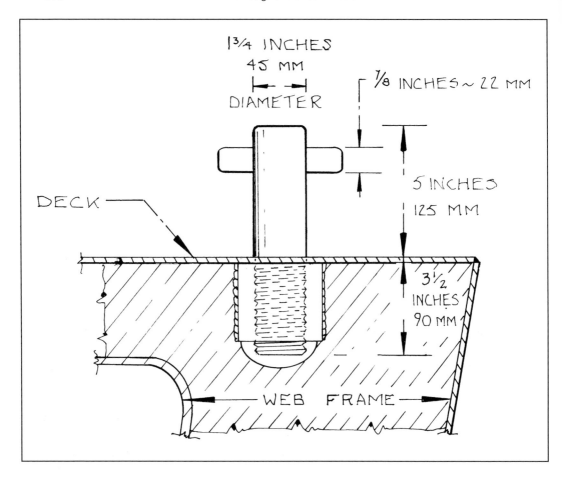

Portable bollard

On boats built for highly competitive racing it is logical to have as few deck fittings as possible. Mooring bollards are only needed when the boat is tied up alongside or being towed to and from a race. During a race they are not only in the way but are also unnecessary weight and windage. The mooring bollard shown in this sketch is the type fitted to the 12-metre *Lionheart*. The bollard, like the rest of the boat, is made of seawater-resistant aluminium alloy and the threaded section is kept well-greased. This threaded section on the bollard screws into a threaded tube welded to a web frame below deck, the tube having thick walls.

CHAPTER 8

Engines

There was a man called Ivan Carr who owned a very beautiful yacht called *Solway Maid*. By way of a tender, apart from the ordinary dinghy, he had a small light runabout with an outboard engine. This was in the days when fast outboard boats were just being developed, and it was found that the fewer people in the runabout the faster she went. The difference between three people aboard and two was very marked. With only the 'driver' aboard, the speed was sensationally increased.

'What we need,' said Ivan to his crew, 'is to try the boat out with no one on board.' The yacht lay in the estuary at Kippford, which was deserted, and sheltered and convenient for this sort of 'experiment'. The outboard boat was brought alongside the *Solway Maid* and the arrangements made. One person held the little boat's bow, another held the stern, and a third leant out from the yacht to start the engine. It was agreed that the petrol would be shut off before the engine was started, so the runabout would only go for a short distance (but, it was hoped, at a tremendous speed) before the engine cut out due to lack of fuel.

'When the engine starts, let go of the bow and stern immediately,' Ivan instructed the helpers. He eased the runabout's bow slightly away from the *Solway Maid* and the outboard engine was started.

The runabout shot off at a considerable speed … but not in a straight line.

'Lucky there is not much petrol in the carburettor and you turned the petrol off,' said Ivan to one of the helpers. 'No! You were going to turn off the petrol,' was the reply. It soon became clear that the arrangements were so elaborate that in the hurley-burley of preparation, no one had turned off the fuel.

Making that characteristic shrieking, waspish buzz which was the hallmark of early high speed outboards, the little boat zig-zagged hither and yon across the river. Whenever her bow pointed in the general direction of the long, glossy magnificent topsides of the *Solway Maid* a profound silence came over the crew. Everyone tried to calculate how big the hole in the hull would be. There was no doubt that the 'experiment' was a success. A suitable outboard runabout unhampered by any human cargo does indeed go quite astonishingly fast.

In time the runabout boat hurled itself into the shallows and slithered a long way over the mud, before stopping!

There is a well-known marine engineering dictum: all marine engines are good; all the faults are in the installations. And, one might add, faults lie in neglect which is almost always worse than over-exuberant experiments with pilotless runabouts.

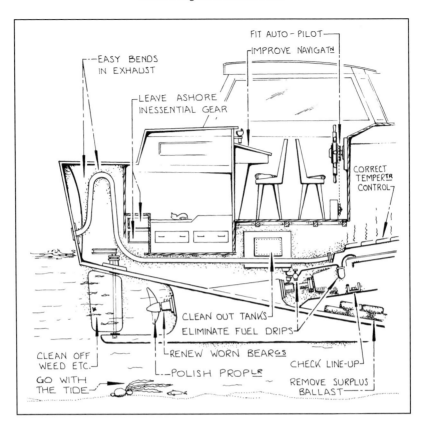

FIT AUTO - PILOT
IMPROVE NAVIGAT^N
EASY BENDS IN EXHAUST
LEAVE ASHORE INESSENTIAL GEAR
CORRECT TEMPER^{TR} CONTROL
CLEAN OUT TANKS
ELIMINATE FUEL DRIPS
CLEAN OFF WEED ETC.
RENEW WORN BEARGS
CHECK LINE-UP
POLISH PROP^{LR}
GO WITH THE TIDE
REMOVE SURPLUS BALLAST

More speed, less fuel

It is usually impossible to get a dramatic increase in speed or saving in fuel by making one addition or alteration to a boat. What is needed is a large number of small improvements, and the elimination of as much resistance as possible. Some improvements, such as getting rid of surplus weight, will give both an increase in speed and a reduction in fuel consumption. Improving the installation, such as a smoothly curved exhaust pipe with no sharp bends, will also increase the engine's performance. If there is no 'rev' counter on the engine it is worth fitting one or borrowing a hand-held one to make sure that the engine is working at near its ideal rpm. If for any reason the peak rpm cannot be reached, then almost certainly the propeller will be the wrong one. The best propellers lose efficiency if the edges are rough, bent or corroded, or if the blades have become pitted or have barnacles on them.

The underside of the keel on all types of boat is often left rough, sometimes with holes where dowels or bedding have fallen out at the fastenings, and sometimes there are protruding fastenings.

In practice, almost always the best way to improve fuel consumption is to navigate carefully, use the tides, keep the engine speed down to its economical level, and steer a straight course.

Exhaust details

So often an engine is properly installed in every detail except the exhaust line. There ought to be a bronze seacock which allows a full flow of exhaust gases, located right at the outlet. If there is no seacock and the exhaust pipe breaks in severe weather, sinking may follow. Admittedly, wise owners carry softwood plugs for this sort of emergency, but it can take a lot of luck for even the most skilful crew to fit a wooden plug up an exhaust pipe outlet in rough weather.

An exhaust pipe should be fully supported, and the one in this sketch should have not only the support at the top but one at the bottom near the drain cock. The drain cock is in a short section of solid pipe between two rubber sections.

Whenever the boat is on moorings, this drain cock should be opened to get rid of any water in the exhaust pipe. Otherwise, as the boat pitches, some water may slop up into the manifold and get into the cylinders.

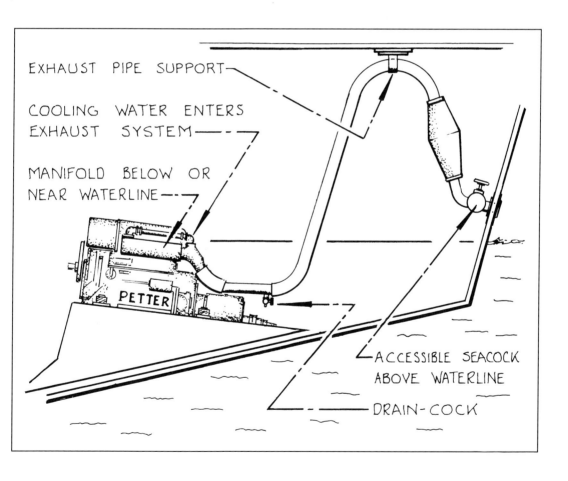

EXHAUST PIPE SUPPORT

COOLING WATER ENTERS
EXHAUST SYSTEM

MANIFOLD BELOW OR
NEAR WATERLINE

PETTER

ACCESSIBLE SEACOCK
ABOVE WATERLINE

DRAIN-COCK

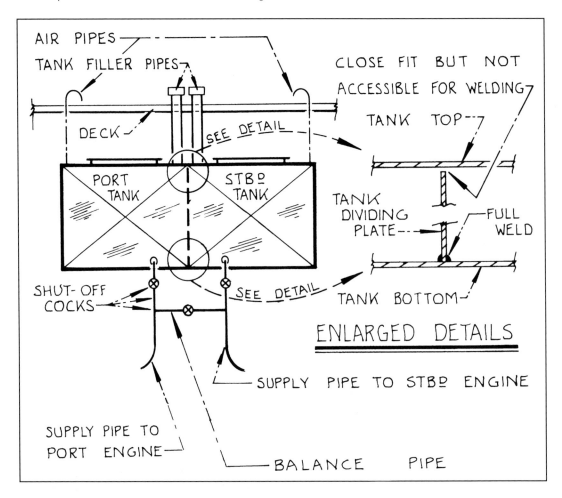

Economical fuel tanks

Any boat with two engines should have two separate fuel tanks. Even if there is only one engine, a very good case can be made for fitting two separate tanks to reduce the risk of polluted or dirty fuel. However, two tanks cost a lot more than one. The type of tank shown here has all the advantages of two tanks, yet is made up like a single one so that there is less cutting and welding, less fabrication time and the price of the tank will be usefully reduced. The centreline division between the two tanks cannot be welded at the top because it is inaccessible when the top of a tank is laid in place. However, this does not matter since water and dirt in fuel sink, so all the pollution is at the bottom and the very tiny opening along the top of the centreline plate is not important. Of course, in some tanks it is possible to get inside through the access hatch on top and weld along the top of the centreline join, but even then making a good weld can be difficult.

   With the supply arrangement shown, one engine is normally run from each tank but if one tank is empty or dirty both engines can be run from one tank via the balance pipe.

Corrosion beater (below)

Propellers, propeller shafts, P-brackets and all the surrounding metal fittings are liable to suffer from corrosion. Their replacement is so expensive that it is well worth spending time and money reducing the risk of corrosion. One way to do this is to fit sacrificial collars onto the propeller shaft. These collars are available from chandlers, and they come in various sizes to fit standard propeller shafts. If the correct size is not available, but the next size down is, it is not difficult to file or drill out the centre hole to fit round the propeller shaft.

The best place to fit a sacrificial collar is just forward of the P-bracket or A-bracket. The gap between the bracket and the propeller should be at most 1 ½ times the shaft diameter, so there should never be space aft of the bracket for the sacrificial collar. Anyone wanting to minimise the disturbance of the water flow to the propeller might machine down the collar to the same diameter as the bottom of the P-bracket and fill the recesses round the nut and bolt end with a suitable stopping material.

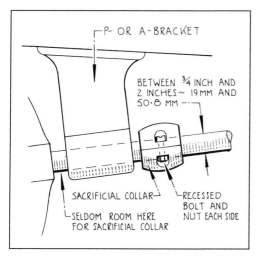

Avoiding fouled propellers (below left)

A boat used for lobster potting, or for any work among submerged ropes, should have a properly guarded propeller, especially if she works close in shore. With an onshore breeze a rope jammed round a propeller can mean a wrecked boat in a matter of minutes.

A propeller guard needs to be elaborate enough to keep away ropes but not so complex that it is expensive or prevents a good flow of water to the propeller. The guard bars which extend fore and aft should not be more than 17° off the angle of water flow or they will cause excessive burbling and loss of speed. So far as possible they should run exactly with the flow of water to the propeller, and they should be as short as possible so that there is no need for stiffening struts at right angles to the stream lines.

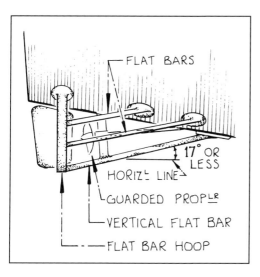

In the sketch the main guard forms the bottom of the P-bracket and goes on to form the heel support of the rudder in association with the flat bar hoop. For a boat which takes the ground this hoop must either be strong enough to support the boat's weight or must be set well above the heel line so that it takes no load when the boat settles on the ground.

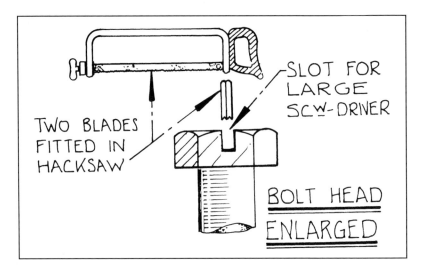

Modifying bolts (above)

Bolts fitted in awkward places can be so very difficult to tighten or loosen. Sometimes it is possible to get the blade of a long screwdriver into an awkward corner where a spanner cannot be used. It is not difficult to change most bolts so that they can be tightened by a screwdriver, though it has to be admitted that the degree of tightening with a screwdriver is sometimes not as good as with a spanner. One way round this is to clamp a Mole grip round the handle of the screwdriver to give extra leverage.

In order to give a good wide slot in the bolt head, two hacksaw blades should be fitted together into the hacksaw frame when the slot in the bolt end is cut, as shown in the sketch.

No fuel in the bilge (opposite)

There is nothing so unpleasant as fuel in the bilge. It floats on top of the bilge water and pollutes everything it touches. If the boat jumps about a lot in a rough sea the fuel is likely to contaminate the cushions, ruin clothes, spread an unpleasant smell which will cause sea-sickness, and leave a grimy high tide mark all-round the boat.

To prevent fuel weeps getting into the bilge there must be some simple sump under fuel taps and filters and any other likely sources of leaks. To make a simple sump, get

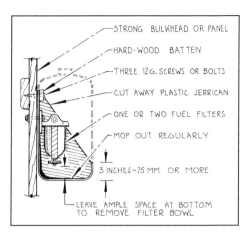

STRONG BULKHEAD OR PANEL

HARD-WOOD BATTEN

THREE 12G. SCREWS OR BOLTS

CUT AWAY PLASTIC JERRICAN

ONE OR TWO FUEL FILTERS

MOP OUT REGULARLY

3 INCHES~75 MM OR MORE

LEAVE AMPLE SPACE AT BOTTOM TO REMOVE FILTER BOWL

hold of a plastic jerry can and cut the top off diagonally. The modified plastic container is fitted under the filter in such a way that even when the boat is heeled any fuel drips will end up in the bottom of the plastic sump. Some people leave newspapers or rags in the bottom of the sump to make mopping up quicker and easier.

The bolts or screws which hold up the sump are kept well up at the top so that there is no chance of a leak through a fastening hole.

An extra fuel tank

On all types of boat there is very often a certain amount of wasted space each side of the engine or engines. Usually there will be some form of walkway so that the engineer can get at the machinery conveniently.

This fuel tank is designed to fit into the awkward space between the outside of the engine bearer and the hull. It will probably be best to make up a mock tank from rough pieces of plywood to be sure that the finished tank will fit in place. The top of the tank is made strong and well supported to carry the weight of as many people as can crowd into the engine space.

It will probably be best to have the draw-off pipe fed through the top of the tank and lead down near the bottom, since any pipe connections at the bottom of the tank are likely to be difficult to reach. It will almost certainly be best to make this sort of tank shorter than the engine space so that one end at least of the tank is accessible.

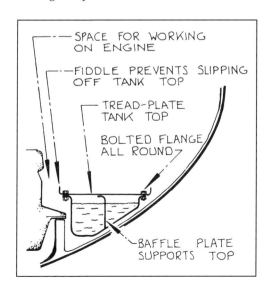

SPACE FOR WORKING ON ENGINE

FIDDLE PREVENTS SLIPPING OFF TANK TOP

TREAD-PLATE TANK TOP

BOLTED FLANGE ALL ROUND

BAFFLE PLATE SUPPORTS TOP

CHAPTER 9

Cabin Furniture

One of the pleasant aspects of yacht surveying is that it opens all sorts of doors. I once surveyed a yacht which had been built totally regardless of expense for an engineering tycoon. The deck saloon curtains extended from deckhead to sole and were of the richest silk with hand painted scenes from old Japan, each picture different yet complimentary to the next. Just drawing the curtains was an adventure and only to be done with clean hands.

The bath, basin and shower taps were of gold, shaped like dolphins cavorting through the waves. The pictures on the walls were originals, immensely valuable and chosen without thought to their setting. To preserve them from the ravages of the salty, damp atmosphere they were sealed in air-tight frames. I'm only selecting just a few of the details to try and give the feeling of this fabulous yacht.

She had a large crew, including more than enough engineers to keep her in immaculate working order, but the owner, who had made his millions as an engineer, enjoyed his trade and did not want to miss his special pleasure while on holiday so he kept his own personal tools in his wardrobe. This clothes stowage room, for it was no mere cupboard, was as big as the cabin of a small cruiser, and was matched by a second similar compartment for his wife's clothes. Inside the owner's clothes cabin there were three leather bags, each with the owner's name stencilled on, each very tough yet elegant and practical, and each filled with metal-working tools.

This is what makes a good yacht so attractive. She is a personal mirror of the owner and his family. It is the furniture and decoration which show the character of boat and owner more than anything else. Now that most boats are semi mass-produced it is good that owners often make their own changes to the standard furniture. It is to be hoped that this trend away from the stereotyped continues, because much modern boat furniture is designed mainly for ease of fabrication. It is not planned to stand up to sea conditions, and sometimes has sharp edges and corners which cause injury in bad weather. Sometimes it even has rapid-rusting steel fastenings and hinges for the very bad reason that these are cheap, and it often has magnetic catches which are useless in a seaway. Cushions held in place by velcro let go when the boat is hurled about, and slippery top surfaces allow mugs, charts, books and match-boxes to slither onto the cabin sole. It is sad that so much furniture is designed to look seductive in a boat show yet is impractical at sea.

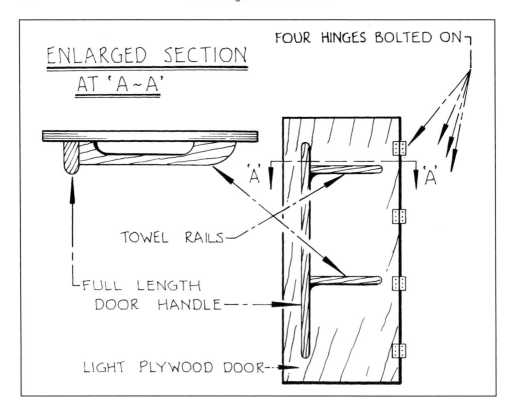

Light strong door (above)

Though this drawing shows the door of a toilet compartment, the ideas illustrated apply to other lightweight doors. No one wants to spend more money than necessary, or carry around unnecessarily heavy furniture and for this reason the door is made of quite thin plywood. This would be too floppy in use in normal circumstances but it is stiffened by four hinges down the side, and by an elegant full length door handle. To strengthen the door horizontally, two towel rails are fitted, glued and screwed to the plywood and to the handle. There should be a minimum of two screws at each end of each towel rail and the hinges should be bolted to the plywood.

Secure steps (opposite, top)

On most boats the cabin steps have to be removed often to get at the engine, the oilskin locker or whatever is fitted aft of the steps. So the foot of the steps needs some secure fixing which is not elaborate but can withstand wear and tear. L-shaped chocks are best and each one must have at least three fastenings. The chocks have to be made of a good quality hardwood with all edges bevelled. They are fitted between the side pieces of the steps to avoid taking up floor space where the crew wish to walk. The height of the chocks should be of the order of 1 inch (25 mm) regardless of the size of the boat.

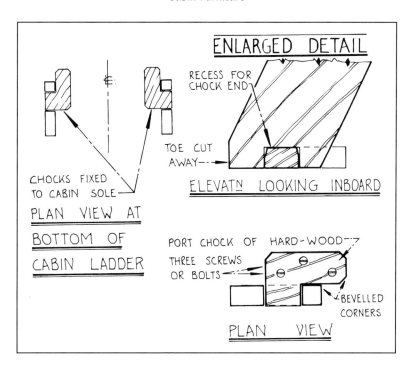

ENLARGED DETAIL

RECESS FOR
CHOCK END

TOE CUT
AWAY

ELEVAT^N LOOKING INBOARD

CHOCKS FIXED
TO CABIN SOLE

PLAN VIEW AT
BOTTOM OF
CABIN LADDER

PORT CHOCK OF HARD-WOOD

THREE SCREWS
OR BOLTS

BEVELLED
CORNERS

PLAN VIEW

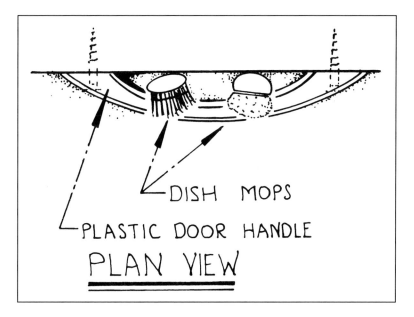

DISH MOPS

PLASTIC DOOR HANDLE

PLAN VIEW

Stowing dish mops (above)

That very simple type of plastic door or drawer handle which has a single screw at each end makes a convenient stowage place for dish mops. The handle can be secured inside a galley locker door, onto the front of the galley work bench or on a nearby bulkhead.

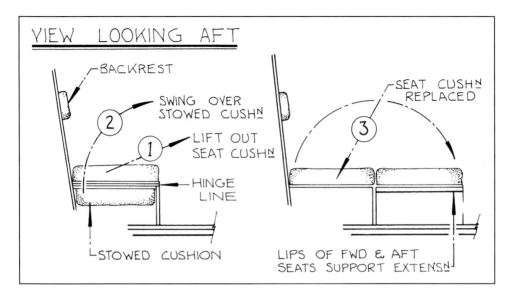

Settee into double berth (above)

Some settees are arranged so that the backrest lifts off and forms a second cushion to make a double berth. However, backrests made wide enough for the second half of a double berth may get in the way of locker and drawer fronts. Also backrests are generally quite thin, 2 inches or 3 inches (50 or 75 mm) being quite common. Berth cushions may be 4 inches or 6 inches (100 or 150 mm) thick for extra comfort. A very convenient way of making a settee into a double berth is by having a portable lift-out cushion, with a hinged cushion underneath as shown stowed on the left hand sketch. To make up the double bunk the seat cushion is lifted out (as shown in arrow 1), then the stowed cushion is swung over on its hinges to the position shown in the right hand sketch, following arrow 2. Finally the seat cushion is placed as shown by arrow 3.

Stowing galley gear (opposite, top)

The top two sketches show a convenient way of keeping a breadboard. The board is made to fit between two beams, with about ⅛ inch (3 mm) clearance each side. Runners are secured to adjacent beams, these runners being about ¾ inch (20 mm) thick. Each runner has a lip on its inner end with a vertical outboard face so that when the boat heels, the breadboard will not slide out of its stowage space.

Pan lids are noisy if stowed loose. It is convenient to have them secured to a galley bulkhead close by the stove and a pair of L-section strips secured onto the bulkhead will hold each pan. So that the pan lids jam tight in place, a short length of semi-soft sponge rubber is glued inside each section to grip the lid.

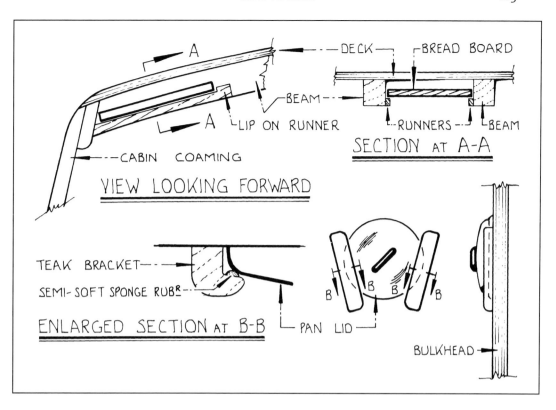

VIEW LOOKING FORWARD

SECTION AT A-A

ENLARGED SECTION AT B-B

Stowage hooks

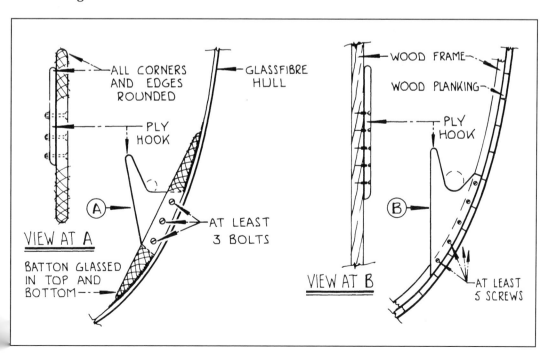

VIEW AT A

VIEW AT B

Ordinary coat hooks are not much use in a boat.

Many of the standard type are too weak for the rough and tumble of life aboard and much of the gear which has to be hung up inside any boat needs a special size of hook. For instance, if a spinnaker pole or whisker pole is stowed below, ordinary coat hooks are not likely to be strong enough for the job. On the left hand side of this sketch, an outsize hook is shown secured inside a fibreglass boat. The first job is to make up a batten of wood to fit the inside of the hull fairly closely. This is glassed in at the top and bottom, probably with three layers of 1 ½ oz. chopped strand mat. Once the batten is firmly hardened in, the hook, which will usually be of plywood, is bolted through.

It may be best to make the hook and the batten together and bolt them together before glassing in the batten.

On the right hand side, the same idea is shown inside a wooden hull, and, of course, it would be similar on a boat built of steel construction.

The hooks are shown as single units but it is quite easy to make up multiple hooks. If for any reason the available plywood is very light, it will be best to make pairs of hooks and secure them to either side of the batten or frame with a solid chock between. Alternatively, several layers of ply can be glued together to give an extra thick hook.

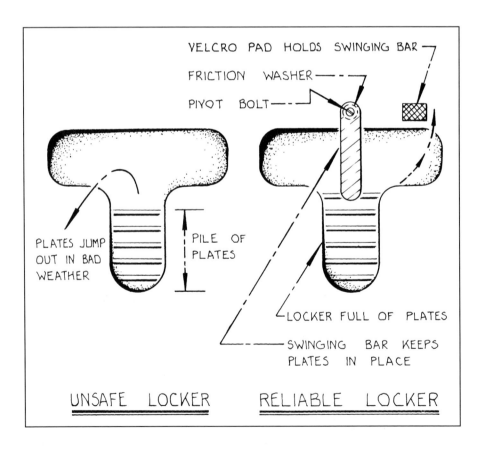

Safe plates (opposite)

There is a common type of plate rack which consists of a locker with an open front. The opening is T-shaped so that the number of plates can be seen easily in the vertical leg of the opening and they can be lifted out of the upper wider part of the opening, as shown on the left. However, this type of opening is not reliable because in very rough conditions the plates can tumble out.

A simple pivot bar of wood, plastic or metal is all that is needed. A friction washer will prevent the bar from swinging sideways and when in harbour the bar can be lodged horizontally, held by a piece of velcro.

Smooth top chart table (below)

Hinges which stand up above the surface of a chart table spoil the surface, and make it difficult to use parallel rulers. In addition, it is sometimes a great nuisance if the chart table top cannot be taken off to look in the chart locker beneath. There is no reason why the top section should be hinged at all. It can be secured by at least two metal strips and chocks, as shown in this section. The drawing board clips can only be used successfully if the chart table edge is the correct thickness, but they are well worth having, especially when sea conditions are rough.

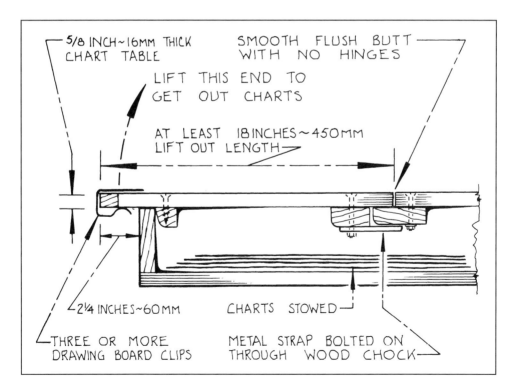

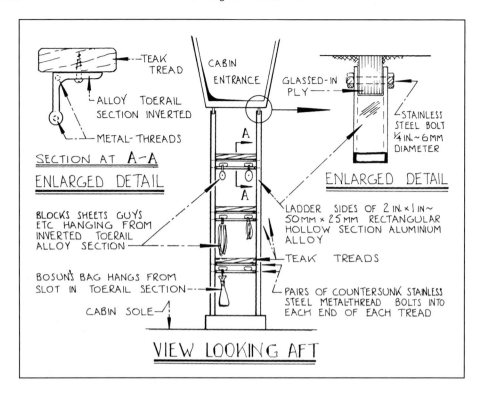

Cabin ladder on a racing boat (above)

This ladder is light yet strong, takes up the minimum space and also acts as a storage rack for all those small items of gear which are often needed in a crisis. Though the ladder shown is built up of aluminium section and teak treads, it could be built from steel and any good quality hardwood. The treads are shown as being made from standard alloy deck edge toerail section turned upside down. However, ordinary aluminium angle bar could be used, welded at each end instead of being secured by metal threads tapped in.

This ladder can be pivoted about the top bolts, the bottom end being swung up to the deckhead. This gives access to the space underneath the cockpit, for engine maintenance and so on.

Ocean cruising details (opposite)

The long-range cruiser Galway Blazer was very carefully thought out by owner and designer in every last detail. The big sketch here is a view looking to starb'd just inside the companionway and shows the skipper's seat. In front of the seat there is a gimballed shelf with very deep fiddles so that a cup with a hot drink in it or even a complete meal can be put down safely. The lockers all round will

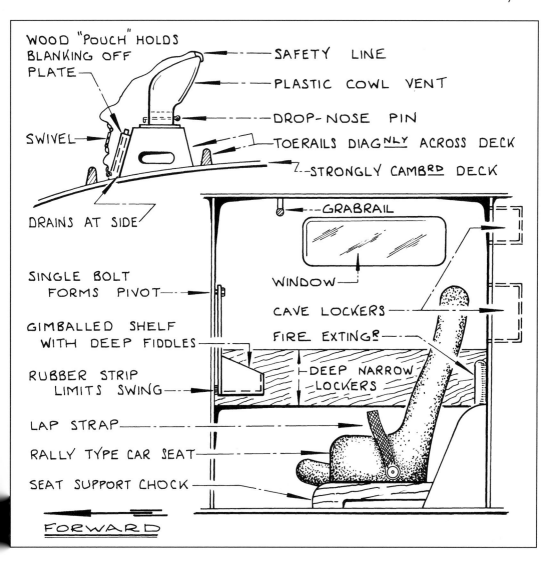

WOOD "POUCH" HOLDS BLANKING OFF PLATE —

SAFETY LINE

PLASTIC COWL VENT

DROP-NOSE PIN

SWIVEL —

TOERAILS DIAG<u>NLY</u> ACROSS DECK

STRONGLY CAMB<u>RD</u> DECK

DRAINS AT SIDE

GRABRAIL

WINDOW —

SINGLE BOLT FORMS PIVOT —

CAVE LOCKERS —

FIRE EXTING<u>R</u> —

GIMBALLED SHELF WITH DEEP FIDDLES —

DEEP NARROW LOCKERS

RUBBER STRIP LIMITS SWING —

LAP STRAP —

RALLY TYPE CAR SEAT —

SEAT SUPPORT CHOCK —

FORWARD

contain everything from tobacco and matches to a torch and reserve torch so that the skipper can spend long hours in comfort with everything he needs close to hand.

The sketch at the top on the left shows the well thought out ventilators which can be swivelled into the wind or locked in one position. In very severe conditions, the cowl can be lifted off and the air inlet sealed off with a special blanking off plate.

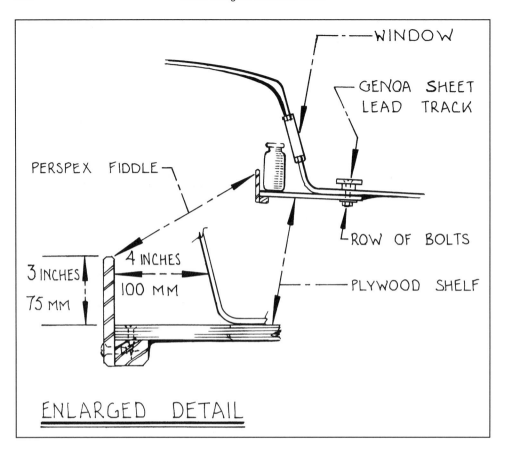

WINDOW

GENOA SHEET LEAD TRACK

PERSPEX FIDDLE

ROW OF BOLTS

3 INCHES

75 MM

4 INCHES

100 MM

PLYWOOD SHELF

ENLARGED DETAIL

Galley shelf

It can be so difficult to add extra storage space in a fibreglass boat, particularly if there are no cheap, convenient fibreglassing facilities available. One way to add a shelf to a galley is to use the row of bolts which hold down the genoa sheet lead track. It may be necessary to fit longer bolts if the existing ones do not extend far enough through the deck.

The dimensions shown in the enlarged detail will fit normal jam jars, spice containers, small bottles and so on. Making the fiddle of Perspex ensures the cook can see what is stored on the handy new shelf.

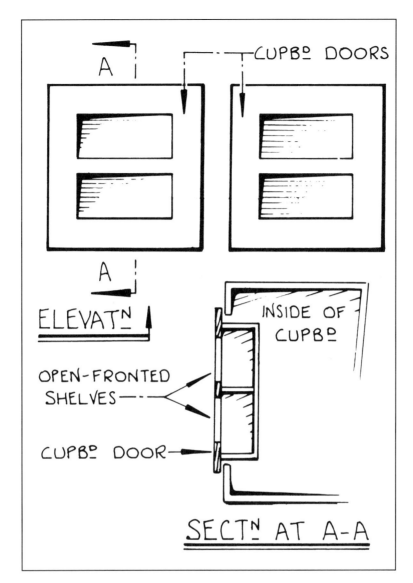

A

CUPB° DOORS

ELEVAT^N

OPEN-FRONTED SHELVES

INSIDE OF CUPB°

CUPB° DOOR

SECT^N AT A-A

Mini lockers and major lockers

Small items of equipment need small lockers, but big pieces of equipment can only be put into large stowage spaces. An ingenious way of making the best use of stowage space is to have double thickness locker doors with open fronted shelves worked into them. This idea looks particularly good if the cupboard doors are in pairs as shown at the top of this drawing. For equipment like torches, flares and matches needed easily to hand, the open fronted shelves are most useful. However, the locker doors must have good hinges and clips to carry the weight and also, of course, to stop the contents of the big cupboards from bursting out in bad weather.

Swinging a starting handle

Some of the various tricks which can be used to give plenty of space to swing an engine starting handle are shown here. For instance, the adjacent front of any furniture like a galley bench can be sloped outboard at the bottom as shown on the left side. Steps or locker doors may be hinged up out of the way, but it is essential to have some form of quick reliable clip to hold them. Instead of a locker door, a curtain may be used provided anything stowed behind it is not going to be in the way. On some boats the starting handle is given an extension but this can be a mixed blessing. For instance, if the extension is long it may be difficult or even impossible for the person winding the handle to reach over and shut down the engine's compression levers. Also a handle on an extension often needs some form of support, and this is unsatisfactory if it takes minutes to rig up with clamps or bolts and so on. Whatever techniques are used, starting the engine by hand should be quick and easy and as nearly effortless as possible.

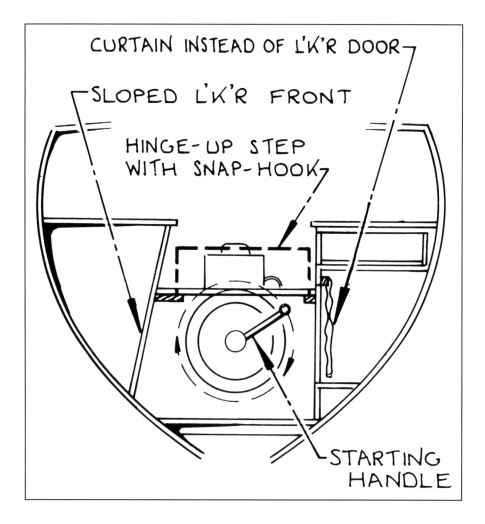

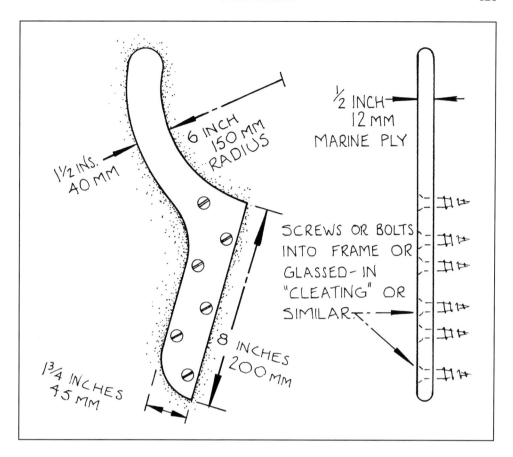

Universal hooks

All sorts of gear have to be stowed in different parts of any boat. Normal coat hooks tend to be too weak for supporting heavy gear and it often pays to make up special hooks. The one shown here will carry sail bags in the fore cabin, tool bags in an engine room, oilskins in their locker and so on.

A row of these hooks made with care and fully varnished not only looks good in any storage place but is extremely useful. The hooks can be fitted in any type of boat: they can be bolted or screwed to wood or metal frames, or they can be screwed to wood hull stiffeners glassed into fibreglass boat. For big boats all the dimensions might be increased by fifty per cent or even doubled.

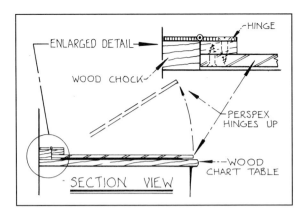

Protected chart table (above)

Charts get damaged in use, particularly if the navigator comes down into the cabin wearing wet oilskins which drip all over the place. One way to protect charts is to have a hinged Perspex cover over the chart table. Some navigators will find it convenient to keep one chart beneath the Perspex and use another one on top.

Another technique which can be used with this type of chart table involves working with special pencils which mark Perspex. Instead of drawing courses and bearings on the chart, they are drawn on top of the Perspex. This is an excellent way of making charts last longer.

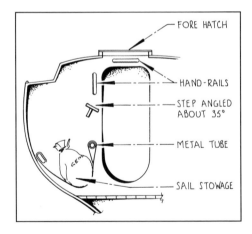

Forehatch steps (above)

When a sailing boat is heeling, it can be surprisingly difficult to get out of a forehatch. The job can be made much easier if steps are angled, and there are plenty of handrails. Admittedly the angled steps make life more difficult when the boat is upright, but then it is usually fairly easy to get through the hatch with the boat either on moorings or sailing upright in light airs.

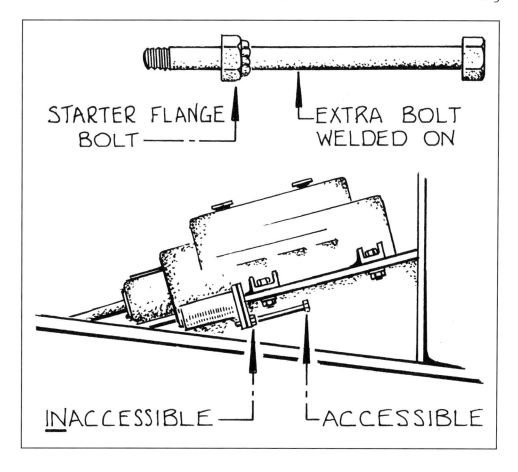

STARTER FLANGE
BOLT

EXTRA BOLT
WELDED ON

INACCESSIBLE

ACCESSIBLE

Improving accessibility

It is quite common to find some bolts are almost impossible to reach on an engine which is installed in a small boat, typically the bolts which hold the starter motor in place. On some craft it is necessary to lift out the whole engine just to get the starter motor out.

One way round this problem is to make the inaccessible bolts extra-long by welding extensions onto their heads. The welded-on bolt may be bigger or smaller in diameter, to fit an available ratchet spanner.

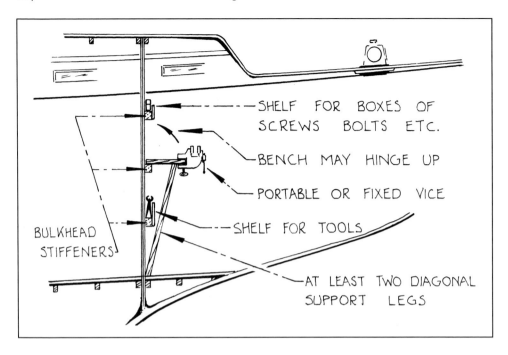

On board workshop

This simple workshop is based on three athwartships bulkhead stiffeners. The top one has a fiddle screwed to it, making it into a shelf for fastenings and small tools. The bottom stiffener has a higher fiddle for larger tools, and the middle one supports a small work bench complete with vice. When not in use, the whole workshop takes up very little space, it does not weigh a great deal, and it will make refitting or any other work on board very much easier.

The work bench must be strongly secured with at least 4 hinges and two props. It should be made of some stout timber such as 1 inch (25 mm) thick hardwood, perhaps with a stiffening batten or fiddle along one edge.

CHAPTER 10

Sails and Cloth Fittings

The most expensive work on a boat is done by electricians. Next in order of costs per man-hour are the engineers, then the shipwrights and boatbuilders. Painters are cheaper, but cheapest of all is work done by sail-makers. There are all sorts of traditional and new reasons why this order of costliness applies, and there are some exceptions, but it does mean that anyone trying to save money can sometimes take advantage of the situation. For instance, it is often far cheaper to make stowage inside a boat out of Terylene, Dacron or synthetic canvas panniers, rather than wood, fibreglass or metal lockers and drawers. 'Cloth furniture' is famous for its low price, speedy manufacture and ease of maintenance.

I once sailed across the Atlantic in a stout old boat which was short of stowage space. To take my clothes and books I had a sail-maker stitch together some rectangular kit bags (using a waterproof cloth) which I screwed up alongside my bunk. At the end of the voyage I removed the bags and put them into a little boat I built myself, giving myself lots of 'instant stowage'.

Furniture and fittings made of cloth do not need painting or varnishing. In winter the cloth items can be taken out of the boat when she has to be cleaned, repainted or mended. Cloth furniture is soft, so if anyone falls against it they suffer no injury. It takes little time to make, and it can be designed to fit the available space; there is no need to accept standard sizes.

Considering that on top of all the other advantages cloth furniture and fittings are lighter than any other type, it is astonishing they are not used more.

Dodgers along the lifelines (overleaf)

These are usually made by a local sailmaker, often from PVC, sometimes from Terylene. For long-range cruising, the dodgers may go right round the stern to give the cockpit the maximum protection.

Sometimes the dodgers serve several purposes; they act as stowage for life rings and have pockets for spare shackles, light line and so on. They can be dangerous if they limit the vision of the crew in the cockpit, so sometimes windows are sewn in.

The bottom sketch shows the way to measure dodgers. It is not enough just to measure the distance between the stanchions because this takes no account of the sheer of the boat. Also the stanchions are not necessarily exactly the same

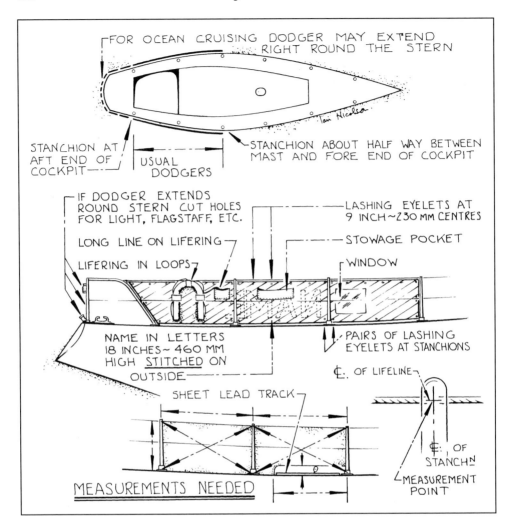

distance apart. To be safe, it is best to measure both port and starb'd sides, and the correct measurements should also be taken for the slots where the headsail sheets go through the genoa sheet lead blocks. It is best to give the sail-maker a very detailed sketch showing the position of every eyelet. Alternatively, the dodgers can be made up and put on board, held temporarily with clothes pegs while the location on each eyelet is marked. The dodgers are then taken back to the sail loft for hammering in the eyelets.

A sail for a gale (opposite)

A headsail on a roller furling forestay is not a good sail to use in very severe conditions. The sail tends to stretch so that its shape is not efficient, and the loading on the various components of the furling gear can become too great, so that a failure occurs.

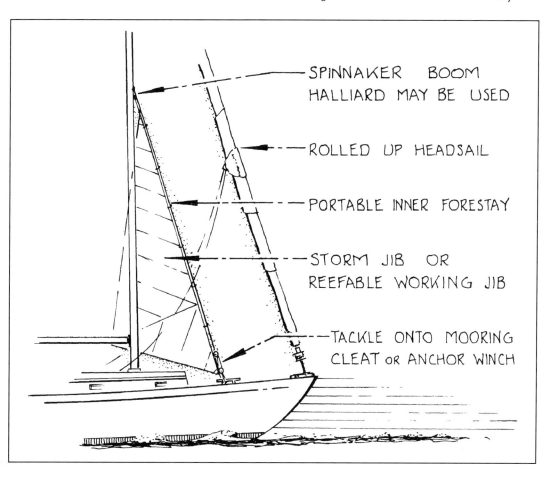

SPINNAKER BOOM HALLIARD MAY BE USED

ROLLED UP HEADSAIL

PORTABLE INNER FORESTAY

STORM JIB OR REEFABLE WORKING JIB

TACKLE ONTO MOORING CLEAT or ANCHOR WINCH

When the wind really pipes up, the ideal headsail is a small, very strongly made jib specially designed for gale conditions. This sail will also be used if the roller headsail becomes torn or damaged. The storm jib does not need much special gear: the spinnaker boom halliard may be used to hoist it up, and the tack can be made fast to a mooring bollard or cleat. It is best not to set this sail flying, but to have a simple portable inner forestay which is set up tight with a four or six part tackle, or a rope lead through a block on the mooring cleat and then to the anchor winch or a winch on the cabin top.

Because this sail is set well aft, it tends to be efficient and easy to handle. It also leaves the fore deck clear for anchor work and should not prevent the crew in the cockpit from seeing forward clearly.

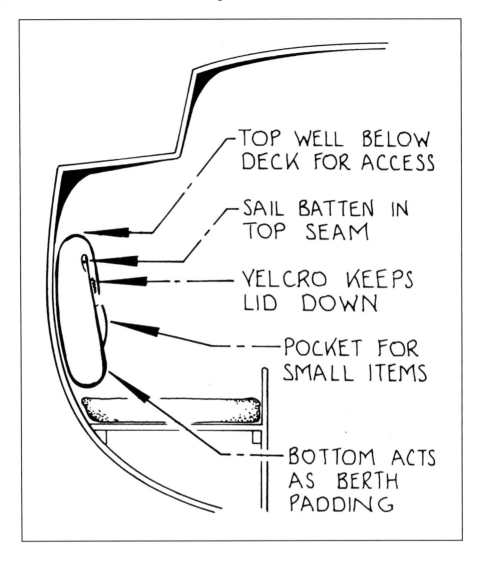

TOP WELL BELOW DECK FOR ACCESS

SAIL BATTEN IN TOP SEAM

VELCRO KEEPS LID DOWN

POCKET FOR SMALL ITEMS

BOTTOM ACTS AS BERTH PADDING

Low price lightweight stowage

Bags for clothes, bosun's stores, bedding or indeed any of the numerous things carried in a boat can be made from the same leathercloth which covers the cushions. On racing boats the bags are sometimes made from a fairly heavy gauge sailcloth, typically 10 oz Terylene or Dacron.

The bags should be made up with bottoms and sides like boxes, and not made flat like envelopes. The top has to be kept down from the deck, otherwise it is very difficult to get anything in and out of a bag. To keep the bag in a good shape, looking smart and easy to use, a sail batten should be sewn into the top inner seam. The outer pocket, or row of pockets, can be so useful for small items like spare shackles, matches, sail needles, twine and so on.

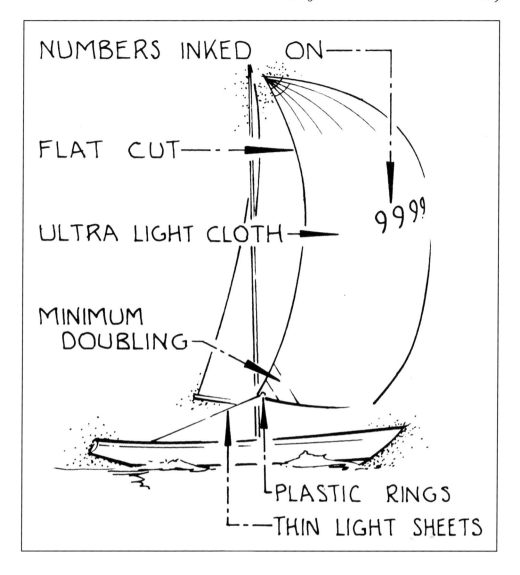

NUMBERS INKED ON

FLAT CUT

ULTRA LIGHT CLOTH

MINIMUM DOUBLING

9999

PLASTIC RINGS

THIN LIGHT SHEETS

A spinnaker for ghosting

In very light conditions a special type of spinnaker is needed. The cloth must be the lightest available, and everything on the sail should be kept down in weight. For instance, instead of having adhesive or stitched-on numbers the figures are put on with ink. Adhesive numbers can be used as a pattern.

The corners are made as light as possible since there is never going to be more than a very gentle strain on this sail. For the same reason the sheets will be light, and this will encourage the crew to take the sail down the minute the wind creeps up to Force 1. Incidentally, it will probably pay to keep the head of the spinnaker forward of the mast and away from the area of dead air caused by the mast and the top of the mainsail.

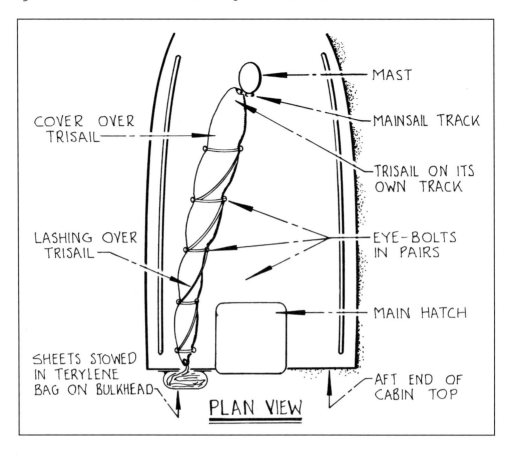

COVER OVER
TRISAIL

LASHING OVER
TRISAIL

SHEETS STOWED
IN TERYLENE
BAG ON BULKHEAD

MAST

MAINSAIL TRACK

TRISAIL ON ITS
OWN TRACK

EYE-BOLTS
IN PAIRS

MAIN HATCH

AFT END OF
CABIN TOP

PLAN VIEW

Trisail for all seasons

The main reason why trisails have become unpopular is the difficulty of setting them in just those conditions when they are needed. When the wind speed gets up into double figures on the Beaufort Scale it is extremely difficult to move about on a boat, let alone get the mainsail off its luff track and engage the slides of a trisail. For ocean cruising, a better arrangement is a separate track up the aft side of the mast beside the main track, used only for the trisail. This track will just go high enough up the mast to accommodate the trisail luff. When not in use the trisail is stowed along the cabin top, permanently secured to the track which goes right down to the deck. It will need a gate probably about 2 or 3 feet (0.7 or 1 metres) above the deck for getting the slides onto the track. The sail is kept with its sheet stowed but secured to the clew and when really bad weather sets in, the mainsail is dropped complete with its boom and lashed down, ideally into a permanent boom gallows. The halliard is then transferred to the trisail, or possibly the trisail may have its own special halliard. Once hoisted, a trisail is normally sheeted to quarter blocks which can double as spinnaker blocks.

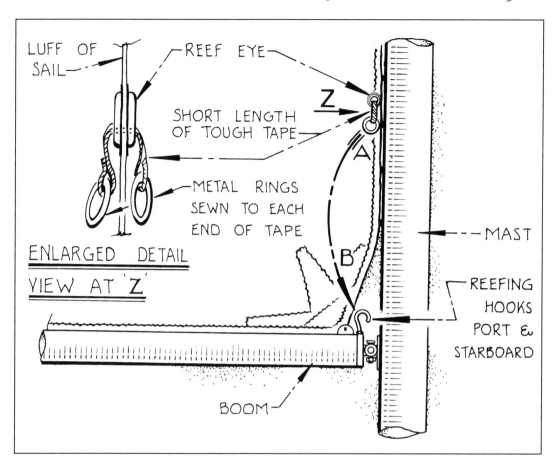

LUFF OF SAIL

REEF EYE

SHORT LENGTH OF TOUGH TAPE

METAL RINGS SEWN TO EACH END OF TAPE

ENLARGED DETAIL VIEW AT 'Z'

MAST

REEFING HOOKS PORT & STARBOARD

BOOM

Easier jiffy reefing

To speed up jiffy reefing the forward reef eyes are fitted with strong lengths of tape threaded through, each end of the tape having a stout stainless steel metal ring. To take in the reefs, the metal ring shown top right at A is slipped over the reefing hook down at B. This is a much easier job than trying to put the reef eye on the sail over the hook. The reason for two metal rings, one on each side of the sail, is that reefing is almost always easier from the windward side and there are normally port and starb'd reefing hooks on the forward end of the boom. So the first reef will go to windward, but when the time comes to pull down another, the vacant hook takes the appropriate ring in the forward eye of the second reef.

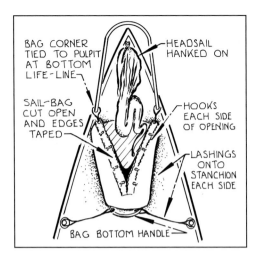

BAG CORNER TIED TO PULPIT AT BOTTOM LIFE-LINE

HEADSAIL HANKED ON

SAIL-BAG CUT OPEN AND EDGES TAPED

HOOKS EACH SIDE OF OPENING

LASHINGS ONTO STANCHION EACH SIDE

BAG BOTTOM HANDLE

Improving sail bags

A standard sail bag can be made easier to use if it is cut down from top almost to the bottom and strong tape sewn either side of the cut. Hooks each side of this new opening are next sewn on and four lashings are put on the bag, two at the bottom and one each side of the new opening. These four lashings hold the bag conveniently in place for setting the headsail or taking it in quickly and neatly. Once the sail is in the bag, the hooks (sometimes call tent hooks) are pulled together with a lashing made from 4-, or 5-, or, on big boats, 6-mm-diameter Terylene line.

The name of the sail should be stencilled in large letters down the side of this new top opening.

Spinnaker chute on a cruiser-racer (opposite)

The advantages of a spinnaker chute are well established. They enable the crew to set and take in the spinnaker with exceptional speed. However, the operation tends to be tough on the sail which as a result is bound to have a shorter life than usual. Also a chute is seldom practical on a boat much over 36 feet (11 metres). Plenty of people would argue that even this size is too big for the effective and regular use of a chute.

Generally speaking, a full length chute permanently fitted inside a boat's cabin is a great nuisance, so the usual technique is to have a fibreglass chute up forward with a flexible tail. The tail is usually made of Terylene sail cloth which is bundled up forward out of the way when not in use. When it is in use it must extend straight aft and for this there must be holes or doorways in the bulkheads.

The length of the chute depends on the length of the folded stowed spinnaker and this sketch shows just about the ultimate limit with the tail of the chute right back in a cockpit locker. The retrieving line is led back round a block and through a fairlead into the cockpit. This enables the helmsman to pull the spinnaker down while steering with the tiller between his knees.

The sheets and halliard all lead out of a forward well, through the front of a carefully rounded pulpit. The sheets and halliard are kept permanently rigged but it may be advisable to have little lashings of rotten cotton holding the ropes clear and neatly stowed while the boat is going to windward.

It may be necessary to have some form of cover over the forward end of the chute to prevent water getting inboard in rough conditions. In very severe conditions two lines of defence are advisable: a good, almost watertight, pair of locker lids over the forward cockpit well, and a tightly fitting cover over the forward end of the chute.

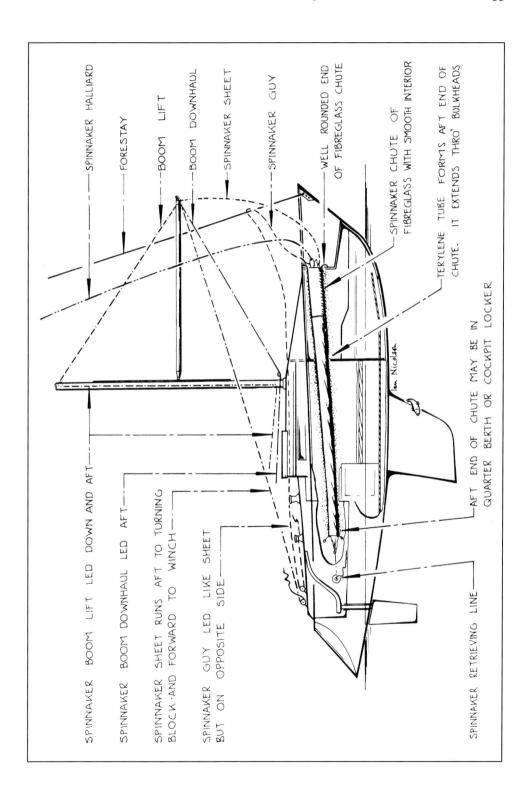

SPINNAKER HALLIARD

FORESTAY

BOOM LIFT

BOOM DOWNHAUL

SPINNAKER SHEET

SPINNAKER GUY

WELL ROUNDED END OF FIBREGLASS CHUTE

SPINNAKER CHUTE OF FIBREGLASS WITH SMOOTH INTERIOR

TERYLENE TUBE FORMS AFT END OF CHUTE. IT EXTENDS THRO' BULKHEADS

SPINNAKER BOOM LIFT LED DOWN AND AFT

SPINNAKER BOOM DOWNHAUL LED AFT

SPINNAKER SHEET RUNS AFT TO TURNING BLOCK·AND FORWARD TO WINCH

SPINNAKER GUY LED LIKE SHEET BUT ON OPPOSITE SIDE

AFT END OF CHUTE MAY BE IN QUARTER BERTH OR COCKPIT LOCKER

SPINNAKER RETRIEVING LINE

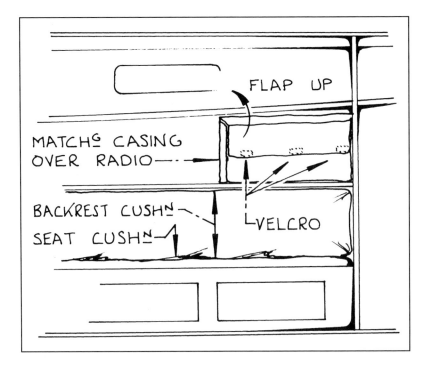

FLAP UP

MATCH<u>S</u> CASING
OVER RADIO—·—

BACKREST CUSH<u>N</u>—
SEAT CUSH<u>N</u>—

└VELCRO

Protecting electrical equipment (above)

Whenever the wind gets up and spray starts to fly, the inside of a boat becomes gradually wetter and wetter. Even big new boats are not immune to this creeping moisture level. Equipment like radios should be protected as much as possible from the weather and one way to do this is to have waterproof plastic casings to fit over them. If the casings can be made to match the settee cushions, the appearance of the cabin and the feeling of comfort will be improved.

It may be necessary to pull polythene bags over the radios and then put the casing on outside, arranging just enough access to the controls to allow the crew to tune in.

This form of casing can also be used for the First Aid outfit, books, navigation equipment and so on.

Gash bin (opposite)

It is awkward trying to cook without a convenient gash bin, but so often there is no convenient space near the galley for one. A portable flexible gash bin may be the answer. It can be made up from any strong waterproof material such as PVC, or even ordinary sail cloth. A local sail-maker will not charge much for this simple bag but if sail cloth is used, ideally it should be tanned so that it will not show the dirt. The whole bag can be taken ashore with the rubbish in for emptying, and when not in use it can be rolled up and stowed in an out of the way locker.

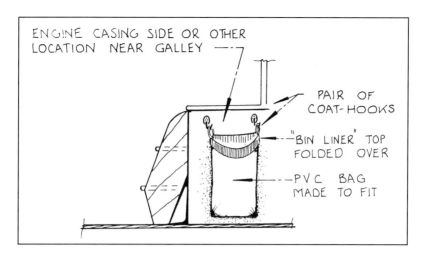

ENGINE CASING SIDE OR OTHER LOCATION NEAR GALLEY

PAIR OF COAT-HOOKS

"BIN LINER" TOP FOLDED OVER

PVC BAG MADE TO FIT

Seagoing bucket (below)

This design of bucket has been proved ideal for a great variety of jobs. It is far better than the kind with a circular base, not least because it can be carried more comfortably without banging against the legs of the person carrying the bucket.

PVC is obtainable from sailmakers and is a better material for the main part of the bucket than canvas.

If copper tacks are not available, galvanised nails can be used instead.

This type of bucket is much stronger than the common plastic bucket and is therefore very useful when the boat is moving fast, and the crew want to scoop up some water to swill down the decks. Under these conditions, plastic buckets tend to break at the handle whereas this bucket is so strong it is more likely to pull the crew overboard!

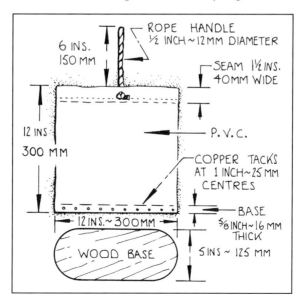

ROPE HANDLE ½ INCH ~ 12MM DIAMETER

6 INS. 150 MM

SEAM 1½ INS. 40MM WIDE

12 INS 300 MM

P.V.C.

COPPER TACKS AT 1 INCH ~ 25 MM CENTRES

12 INS. ~ 300MM

BASE ⅝ INCH ~ 16 MM THICK

5 INS ~ 125 MM

WOOD BASE

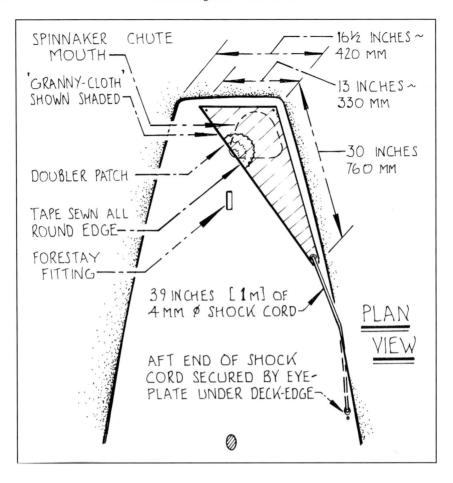

Granny cloth

All sorts of racing boats are now using spinnaker chutes. Perhaps the chief disadvantage of a chute is that it lets in a lot of water when going to windward in severe conditions. The trouble can be minimised by the fitting of a cloth cover over the entrance of the chute. This cover is sometimes known as a 'granny cloth'.

The sketch shows one on a Fireball dinghy, but the idea can be used on virtually any boat with a chute.

The doubler patch is needed to prevent the sail chafing the granny cloth badly as it goes in and out. In settled conditions, when winds are light, the whole granny cloth might be removed to make spinnaker handling quicker and easier.

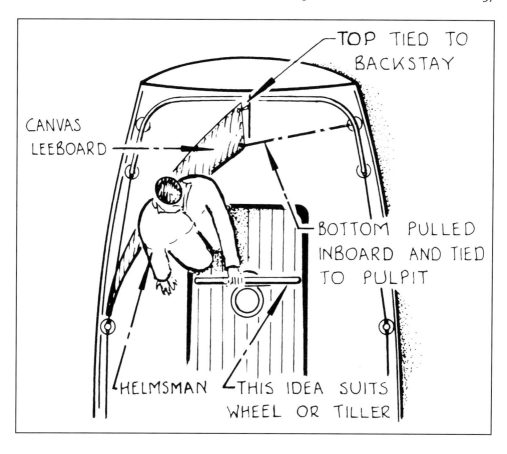

TOP TIED TO BACKSTAY

CANVAS LEEBOARD

BOTTOM PULLED INBOARD AND TIED TO PULPIT

HELMSMAN

THIS IDEA SUITS WHEEL OR TILLER

For comfort and protection

There is nothing so uncomfortable as the open cockpit of a small yacht in big seas. One way to improve things for the helmsman is to give him something comfortable to lean back on, such as a leeboard high enough to support his shoulders. If this cloth backrest can also be designed to keep some of the wind and rain and spray off him, so much the better. The leeboard shown here is only drawn in for the starb'd side, but it can either be moved across when the boat is making very long tacks as on an ocean cruise, or, for inshore work, two leeboards may be fitted, one each side.

CHAPTER 11

Maintenance and Improvements

I have a friend who hates maintenance work. He used to get over the problem by buying a new boat each year, and trading the old one in. This became expensive, but by luck his daughters were then old enough to help him with the refitting work. Just when they began to lose enthusiasm for refurbishing boats, they gained a strong interest in men, so my friend found himself with sons-in-law to do his boat maintenance work. It is one way of getting over the problem.

In contrast, another of my friends liked nothing about boats except the renewal work. He would buy some run-down old collander and lovingly bring her back to shining glory. I'd meet him looking dejected and he would tell me that there was nothing left to do on his current boat. This sadness seldom lasted long, because someone always came along, saw the boat and fell in love with her, and my friend made a useful profit. He would then look around for a slightly bigger boat in dilapidated condition and away he went again ...

I've lost touch with him, but as each boat was bigger than his previous one, I calculate that by now he owns a 150-footer ... and by the time he has finished fitting her out, the work he did first will need redoing, so he'll be happy all the time.

This chapter, like the others in the book, is a random gathering of ideas I've collected from all over the world for refitting and improving boats, and making them more fit for voyaging.

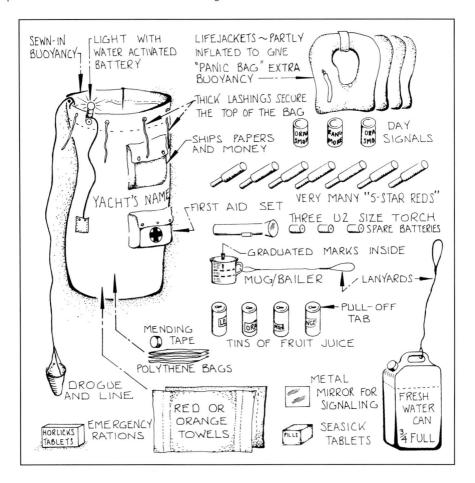

Panic bag

Perhaps the most important item on any boat going far offshore is the panic bag. It is stowed in a cockpit locker, or near the main cabin entrance, and it is packed with everything needed when the boat is abandoned.

The panic bag is designed to float when thrown overboard but it has a drogue and line to prevent it drifting off to leeward. The line may be used to secure the panic bag to the life raft. Inside the panic bag, apart from such equipment as flares and emergency food, there will be at least one water can, and on an ocean cruiser other water cans will be stowed in the cockpit. All these cans are filled three-quarters full so that they will float, and they can be tied to the life raft or, if there is plenty of space, put inside it once the life raft is inflated. Everything in the panic bag should be waterproof, or very carefully wrapped in waterproof polythene bags. Equipment like torches and flares, being vulnerable, is wrapped in the towelling, or padded round with the lifejackets.

The panic bag itself should be made of bright orange material such as PVC or Terylene so that it can be used to wave and attract attention.

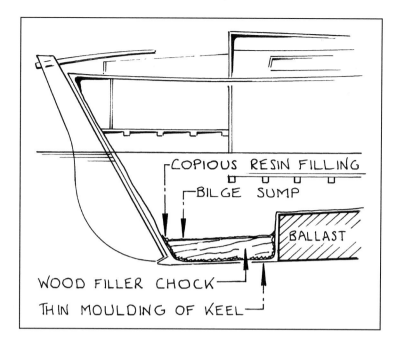

Going aground safely

On modern boats which have deep fibreglass keels, the aft end of the keel is often the bilge sump. When the bilge water runs down into the sump at the bottom, it is only separated from the sea by the thickness of the fibreglass shell. When this type of boat runs aground she may chafe the heel of the keel and before long a hole will appear, whereupon the boat fills and sinks.

Anyone with this sort of boat can make her much safer simply by filling the bottom of the sump with a wooden chock perhaps 8 inches (200 mm) deep, well glassed in all round. The chock has to be a fairly good fit and bedded down on wet glass, with more glassing and copious resin put on top of the wood chock. Now when the boat runs aground she has to chafe right through the full depth of the wood chock before the watertight integrity of the hull is pierced.

Winter lay up (overleaf)

It is easy to forget some of the important jobs which should be done on every boat every winter when she is laid up. Quite apart from the obvious jobs like cleaning and repainting, this is the time to get spares, to grease parts which are awkward to reach, to look at basic structure like ballast keel bolts, and to get rid of puddles of oil, water, and fuel which may have dripped down into the bilge.

Safety equipment needs checking every year because most of the time when afloat it is not used and is therefore neglected. Life jackets, especially the inflatable type,

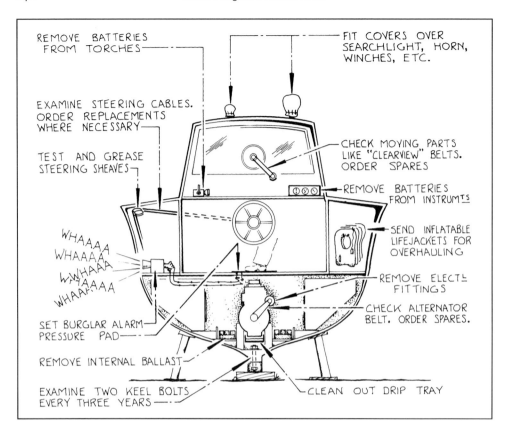

REMOVE BATTERIES FROM TORCHES

FIT COVERS OVER SEARCHLIGHT, HORN, WINCHES, ETC.

EXAMINE STEERING CABLES. ORDER REPLACEMENTS WHERE NECESSARY

CHECK MOVING PARTS LIKE "CLEARVIEW" BELTS. ORDER SPARES

TEST AND GREASE STEERING SHEAVES

REMOVE BATTERIES FROM INSTRUM^TS

WHAAAA WHAAAAA WHAAAA WHAAAAA WHAAAAA

SEND INFLATABLE LIFEJACKETS FOR OVERHAULING

REMOVE ELECT^L FITTINGS

CHECK ALTERNATOR BELT. ORDER SPARES.

SET BURGLAR ALARM PRESSURE PAD

REMOVE INTERNAL BALLAST

EXAMINE TWO KEEL BOLTS EVERY THREE YEARS

CLEAN OUT DRIP TRAY

have a relatively limited life and should be inspected by an expert. If this cannot be done they should be blown up and left for three or four days to see if the air leaks out. An occasional test by immersion in a bath, or better still a practice life-saving session in a swimming bath, will show if a life jacket is up to its job.

Safely laid up (opposite)

Each year boats are damaged while lying ashore because of inadequate cradles and poor protection from the weather. The left hand side of this drawing shows common features found on bad cradles. It is not unusual, for instance, to see fibreglass hulls pushed in noticeably at one or two of the support legs of a cradle. This can cause damage not only to the hull but to the bulkheads, furniture inside the hull and so on.

If there are metal eyes on a tarpaulin these will scratch the topsides when the wind blows. For this reason lashings should be kept tight and the eyelets well below the waterline where they will either be clear of the hull, or at least will not spoil the topside gel coat.

Better techniques are shown on the right hand side of the drawing. Here not only is there a broad strong cradle but also a goal-post is secured over the top of the boat with the cross beam lashed to the chain-plates.

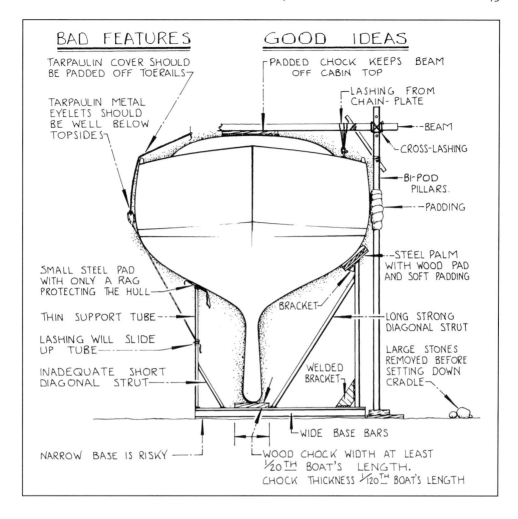

BAD FEATURES

TARPAULIN COVER SHOULD BE PADDED OFF TOERAILS

TARPAULIN METAL EYELETS SHOULD BE WELL BELOW TOPSIDES

SMALL STEEL PAD WITH ONLY A RAG PROTECTING THE HULL

THIN SUPPORT TUBE

LASHING WILL SLIDE UP TUBE

INADEQUATE SHORT DIAGONAL STRUT

NARROW BASE IS RISKY

GOOD IDEAS

PADDED CHOCK KEEPS BEAM OFF CABIN TOP

LASHING FROM CHAIN-PLATE

BEAM

CROSS-LASHING

BI-POD PILLARS.

PADDING

STEEL PALM WITH WOOD PAD AND SOFT PADDING

BRACKET

LONG STRONG DIAGONAL STRUT

LARGE STONES REMOVED BEFORE SETTING DOWN CRADLE

WELDED BRACKET

WIDE BASE BARS

WOOD CHOCK WIDTH AT LEAST $\frac{1}{20}$TH BOAT'S LENGTH.
CHOCK THICKNESS $\frac{1}{120}$TH BOAT'S LENGTH

Wide webbing (overleaf)

It is easy to buy strong wide webbing, because chandlers sell it for dinghy toestraps. This webbing has many uses afloat by virtue of its strength, because it does not rot, and because it can be sealed with a hot knife or hot skewer to prevent the ends unravelling.

The most obvious use for webbing is as stowage for pencils above a chart table, but the same arrangement can be used for stowing tools beside an engine.

On deck, equipment like anchors and spinnaker poles can be secured beneath a well fastened loop of webbing which, when the gear is in use, lies flat so that the crew can walk about on top of it without damage to themselves or to the webbing. Perhaps its most valuable use is as hinges. Hatch hinges and even cabin door hinges tend to get broken if a boat is used hard year after year. As hatch hinges, webbing has the great advantage that it can allow a hatch top to fold right back through more

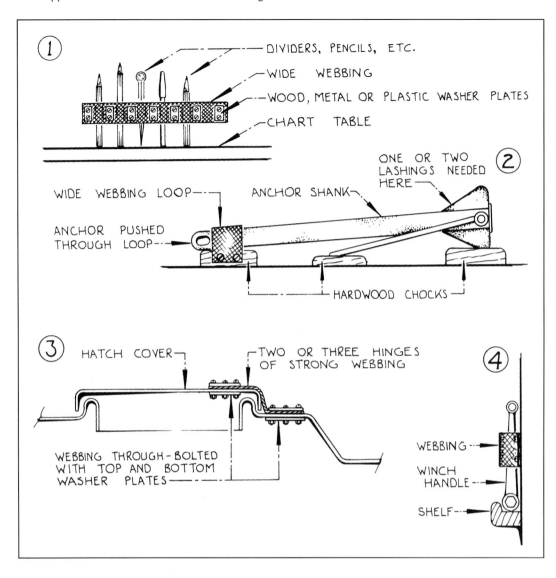

① DIVIDERS, PENCILS, ETC.
— WIDE WEBBING
— WOOD, METAL OR PLASTIC WASHER PLATES
— CHART TABLE

② ONE OR TWO LASHINGS NEEDED HERE
WIDE WEBBING LOOP
ANCHOR SHANK
ANCHOR PUSHED THROUGH LOOP
HARDWOOD CHOCKS

③ HATCH COVER
TWO OR THREE HINGES OF STRONG WEBBING
WEBBING THROUGH-BOLTED WITH TOP AND BOTTOM WASHER PLATES

④ WEBBING
WINCH HANDLE
SHELF

than 180°. Each end of each hinge must be securely bolted with metal backing plates or washer plates. There should be at least three bolts at each end of each hinge.

The fourth sketch bottom right shows a typical stowage problem solved, and the same technique can be used in the galley for cooking utensils.

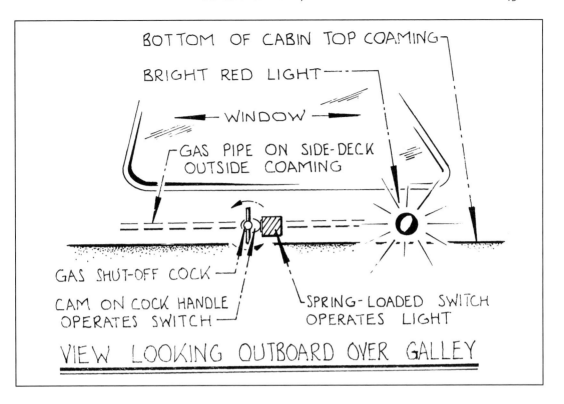

BOTTOM OF CABIN TOP COAMING

BRIGHT RED LIGHT

WINDOW

GAS PIPE ON SIDE-DECK OUTSIDE COAMING

GAS SHUT-OFF COCK

CAM ON COCK HANDLE OPERATES SWITCH

SPRING-LOADED SWITCH OPERATES LIGHT

VIEW LOOKING OUTBOARD OVER GALLEY

Bottled gas safety

The ideal place to locate a gas bottle is out on deck, so that any leaks will go overboard. But if a gas bottle is on deck, someone has to go out to shut off the cock when cooking is finished. However, if the gas pipe is run along the side deck close up against a cabin coaming, the shut-off cock can extend through the coaming. To warn everyone that the gas is switched on, a cam is fitted on the cock handle so that it makes contact with a spring-loaded electric light switch and a bright red light shines over the cooker. Not only is this a good safety device, but it also encourages everyone on board to save gas.

For long-range cruising

Years ago the majority of yachts were capable of deep sea cruising, but few went far offshore. Now few yachts are truly suitable for off-soundings cruising, yet many go.

   If a standard production yacht, or indeed any craft, is to be taken far offshore she should be modified and prepared for the worst the weather can do. Some of the changes are shown here. Many are cheap and easy to fit, but it can be difficult to change the windows. It may pay to fit an entirely new extra strong cabin top, or completely change the existing one. Eliminating large windows is one of the ways a boat is made able to stand up to severe conditions, but everything on deck should be made gale-proof. Where possible, gear should be taken below.

   Standard size fittings like jib hanks, blocks, shackles, stanchions, lifelines, sheet winches and even the tiller should be removed and replaced with fittings two sizes bigger. It is rare for rigging to fail, but not uncommon for shackles and other link pieces to give trouble. It is unusual for cleats and other fixed parts to fail, but common for rudders, goose-necks and other moveable components to give problems.

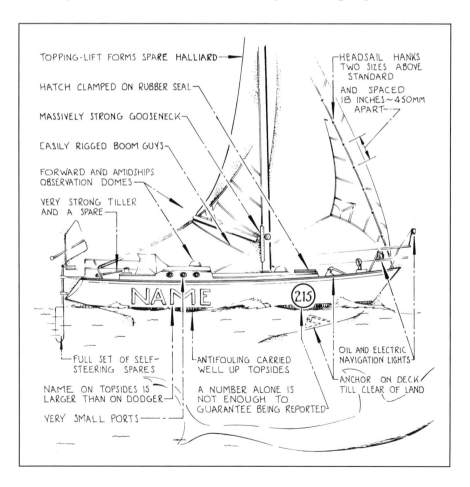

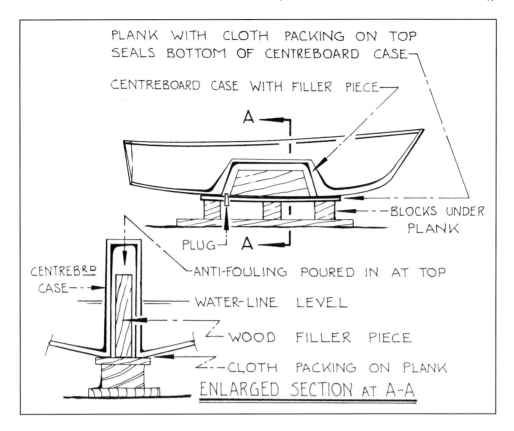

PLANK WITH CLOTH PACKING ON TOP SEALS BOTTOM OF CENTREBOARD CASE

CENTREBOARD CASE WITH FILLER PIECE

A

BLOCKS UNDER PLANK

PLUG   A

CENTREBRD CASE

ANTI-FOULING POURED IN AT TOP

WATER-LINE LEVEL

WOOD FILLER PIECE

CLOTH PACKING ON PLANK

ENLARGED SECTION AT A-A

Painting inside a centreboard case

The painting of the inside of a centreboard case by using a brush on a long stick is unsatisfactory. The paint is not put on thickly, and not at all in some corners. A much better way is shown here. The bottom of the case is sealed tight by placing a plank along the bottom slot after the centreboard has been taken out. The keel chocks force the plank up against the hull as the chocks at the bow and stern are taken away. Antifouling paint is poured in at the top of the case, till it extends up to above the load waterline. So that a vast amount of paint is not needed, a wood filler piece is put inside the case to take up some of the empty space. When the paint has well penetrated all the corners, the bung in the sealing plank is withdrawn and the paint poured out into a tin.

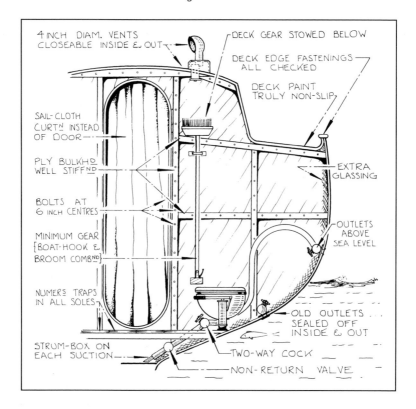

4 INCH DIAM. VENTS CLOSEABLE INSIDE & OUT

DECK GEAR STOWED BELOW

DECK EDGE FASTENINGS ALL CHECKED

DECK PAINT TRULY NON-SLIP

SAIL-CLOTH CURT? INSTEAD OF DOOR

PLY BULKHD WELL STIFFND

EXTRA GLASSING

BOLTS AT 6 INCH CENTRES

OUTLETS ABOVE SEA LEVEL

MINIMUM GEAR [BOAT-HOOK & BROOM COMBND]

NUMERS TRAPS IN ALL SOLES

OLD OUTLETS ... SEALED OFF INSIDE & OUT

STRUM-BOX ON EACH SUCTION

TWO-WAY COCK

NON-RETURN VALVE

Offshore cruiser

The ideas shown here are for a cruiser which is to be used for long-range sailing. For instance, all the ventilators should be at least 4 inches in diameter, otherwise they tend to be ineffective in light winds or hot climates. Nevertheless, they should be designed so that they can be closed both on the inside and the outside with the onset of bad weather. In gale conditions, no gear should be on deck since it is liable to be washed overboard and it may get in the way of the crew. That is why the deck broom (which incidentally is also the boathook) is stowed out of the way in the toilet compartment.

This compartment has a sailcloth curtain instead of a door partly to improve ventilation, partly to save weight, and also because the sailcloth can, in an emergency, be used for patching the sails. It also has the advantage that it is unlikely to cause injury to anybody in bad weather, whereas a slamming door can hurt.

The bulkhead has been fully stiffened, and this is something which is most important if the boat was originally built for coastal cruising. A typical cheap production yacht needs quite a lot of beefing up before it is taken on a deep sea voyage.

Many production yachts do not have accessible bilges and it may be necessary to cut the cabin sole right out and fit a new one with numerous traps.

For offshore work even quite a small boat should have three bilge pumps. One of them can be the toilet outlet pump provided there is a non-return valve in the suction line and a good large two-way cock. All the discharge points in the hull should be above the load-water line so that a bung can be driven in if the seacock fails. The toilet outlet will normally be kept down in the boot-top and may have a loose PVC cover over the top, down to the waterline.

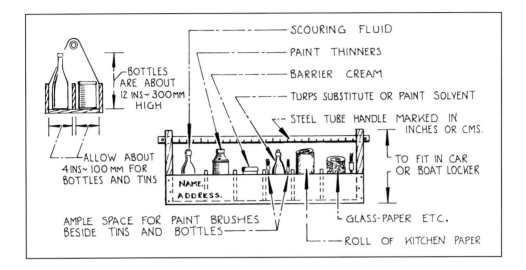

Tool box (above)

This specially made box is for use during the laid-up period, or on a big boat which carries a comprehensive set of tools and maintenance equipment. It is made to fit inside the owner's car, or in a locker aboard. The carrying handle has a split pin at each end to prevent it slipping out and acts as a spare rule.

Some people will make up two of these boxes, one for paints and so on and the other for tools. The end pieces will probably be about ¾ inch (20 mm) thick but ½ inch (12 mm) material will do for the sides and bottom. The divisions can be made of quite light material but the overall length should not exceed 3 feet (1 metre) or the whole box will get too heavy to carry.

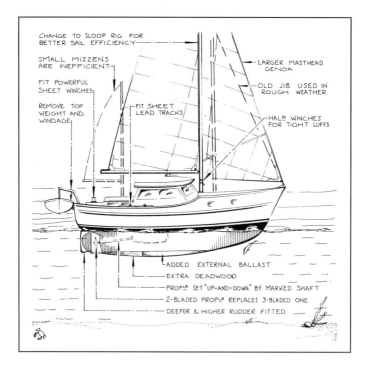

Labels within the illustration:

CHANGE TO SLOOP RIG FOR BETTER SAIL EFFICIENCY

SMALL MIZZENS ARE INEFFICIENT

FIT POWERFUL SHEET WINCHES

REMOVE TOP WEIGHT AND WINDAGE

FIT SHEET LEAD TRACKS

LARGER MASTHEAD GENOA

OLD JIB USED IN ROUGH WEATHER

HAL⁰ WINCHES FOR TIGHT LUFFS

ADDED EXTERNAL BALLAST

EXTRA DEADWOOD

PROP⁰ SET 'UP-AND-DOWN' BY MARKED SHAFT

2-BLADED PROP⁰ REPLACES 3-BLADED ONE

DEEPER & HIGHER RUDDER FITTED

Faster cruising under sail

Even people who are not interested in racing like to make reasonable progress and not waste unnecessary time at sea. Boats built as motor sailers are sometimes very disappointing under sail, simply because they have too many disadvantages. Some power boats are helpless under sail and yet with a few modifications could be made to go reasonably well.

Not all the ideas shown here can be worked in to any particular boat, but it is amazing what a difference comes about if the majority of these changes are made carefully and accurately.

To get the very best out of a boat it is usually necessary to call in a naval architect, but even without his help a lot can be done if good sails are well set, with halliard and sheets properly tightened in.

A three-bladed propeller is a great drag whereas a two-bladed one carefully aligned behind the stern-post does not give anything like as much resistance. A good rudder, properly shaped and with no sharp outstanding flanges, will improve steering and make the boat more pleasant to handle. Apart from other advantages it will also ensure that she handles better in enclosed waters. For improved windward performance, there is one simple rule which should always be followed: go up as much as possible and down as much as possible. This means the rig should be as high as practical even if it is shorter fore and aft, and in the same way there should be as much depth of keel as can be conveniently arranged. The deep keel need not extend fore and aft for any distance at all, as is seen on racing dinghies where centre-plates are quite narrow at the bottom but always deep.

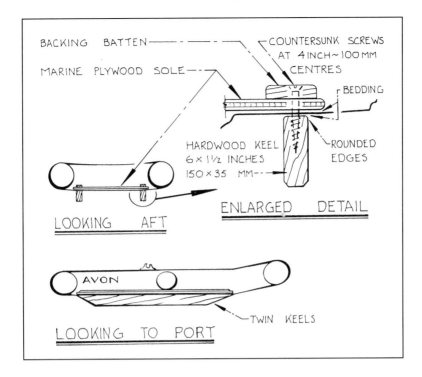

BACKING BATTEN
COUNTERSUNK SCREWS AT 4 INCH~100 MM CENTRES
MARINE PLYWOOD SOLE
BEDDING
HARDWOOD KEEL 6 × 1½ INCHES 150 × 35 MM
ROUNDED EDGES

ENLARGED DETAIL

LOOKING AFT

AVON
TWIN KEELS

LOOKING TO PORT

Longer life for inflatables

Inflatable dinghies are widely popular because they are easy to carry, they do not chafe the hull of any boat they rub alongside, for their overall length they are cheap, and so on. They do have one disadvantage, namely that they are not tough enough to stand up to being dragged ashore, particularly where the ground is rough. If they are fitted with a pair of hardwood keels bolted or screwed through, the life of the boat will be greatly extended. Though the keels need not be as deep as 6 inches (150 mm), this depth will make sure that even on really rocky coasts the dinghy should have a long life. For minimum weight it might be better to fit three or even four keels only 1 inch (25 mm) deep and ¾ inch (20 mm) wide.

Going far offshore

Though lots of standard production boats are taken on long voyages, the majority of them are not suitable for deep-sea long-range cruising. However, quite a few of these boats can be made into ocean cruisers with the expenditure of money, time and effort.

A popular rig for long-range sailing is the ketch and it is often possible to change from sloop to ketch, even on a standard production boat. The next job is to make the boat safe on deck, and this means getting rid of big vulnerable windows and fitting small ports which can be opened in hot weather. In the same way if the cockpit is large, it should be partly decked over. All the deck fittings have to be made extra rugged; this usually means throwing away the very weak fittings, putting the cockpit cleats in place of the small cleats on the mast and fitting really big cleats on the cockpit coamings and at the mooring points on the fore deck and aft deck.

Before going far offshore, the boat has to be pictured in the very worst weather so that every bit of equipment is made well able to stand up to rough conditions and the general run of accidents afloat. For instance, alternators seem to be less reliable than the old-fashioned dynamo, so a change might be made to the engine. Engine spares will be needed and in practice it is generally better to have a small reliable diesel which will go on running in all conditions, using very little fuel rather than a big engine which will be heavy on fuel and spares, take up a lot of weight, and occupy a lot of useful space. Added to which, the small diesel is normally easier to maintain with more space round it.

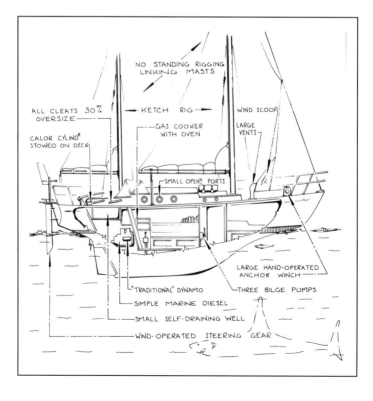

Curing leaks

There are certain well-established principles for stopping leaks. The most important is that work must be done on the outside, regardless of whether the leak is above or below the waterline.

Another principle is that the leak stopping must be applied with some force. For instance, in this sketch the Sylglas tape is forced against the coaming and deck by close spaced screws through a stout wooden batten. Any material used for stopping leaks should remain flexible and should not harden, otherwise when the boat moves slightly the material is likely to allow water to seep down between the structure and the bedding compound. Sylglas tape remains tacky throughout its life and sticks to whatever it is pressed against.

Another principle of leak stopping is that the work should not be started until the whole area has been fully dried out. Once the job has been completed, it is sensible to test it by turning a hose on while someone goes inside the vessel with a bright light to make sure no water seeps in.

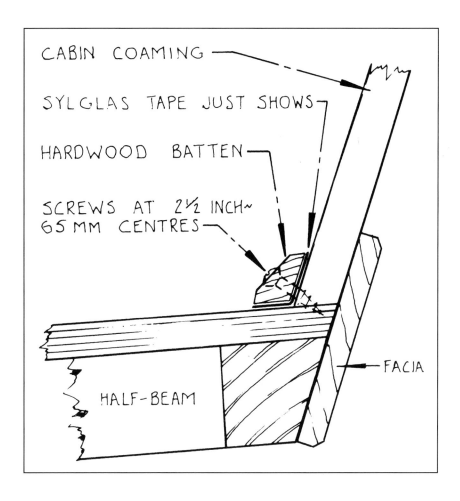

CABIN COAMING

SYLGLAS TAPE JUST SHOWS

HARDWOOD BATTEN

SCREWS AT 2½ INCH~ 65 MM CENTRES

FACIA

HALF-BEAM

A cruising boat from a racer

Some interesting cruising boats are owned by people who have bought outclassed racing machines and modified them. Apart from the obvious additional internal stiffening around areas like the mast pillars, P-bracket, cabin sole bearers and so on, there are quite a few alterations needed on deck and below. Most of these are easy changes which will not be found difficult by a competent amateur shipwright. The sails will need some alterations, for instance it may pay to cut down the area of the mainsail, and perhaps get rid of the biggest genoas and spinnakers. A storm jib will certainly be needed and this can sometimes be set in an inner forestay so that it is well inboard, easy to set and take in, and can be sheeted well aft so that extra sheet lead blocks are not going to be needed. One advantage of setting a storm jib on an inner forestay is that it can be put up before the headsail on the main jib stay is taken in.

Equipment for mooring up and tieing alongside will need augmenting, and the cockpit will need attention. A hood over the companionway extending right out to the cabin-top coaming sides will give shelter to the cockpit. Wherever the cockpit coamings have been chipped and damaged, they can be sheathed over with teak which will also improve the appearance of the boat. Finally, the engine should be made totally reliable and it often pays to change the folding feathering propeller to a fixed one to get better performance under power, especially when going astern.

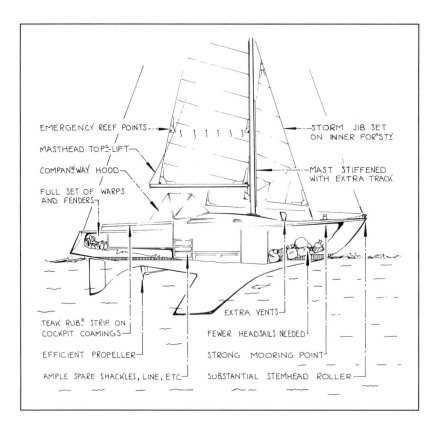

EMERGENCY REEF POINTS

MASTHEAD TOPS-LIFT

COMPANNWAY HOOD

FULL SET OF WARPS AND FENDERS

STORM JIB SET ON INNER FOR'STY

MAST STIFFENED WITH EXTRA TRACK

TEAK RUBR STRIP ON COCKPIT COAMINGS

EFFICIENT PROPELLER

AMPLE SPARE SHACKLES, LINE, ETC

EXTRA VENTS

FEWER HEADSAILS NEEDED

STRONG MOORING POINT

SUBSTANTIAL STEMHEAD ROLLER

No ropes round the prop

It is all too easy to catch a rope round a boat's propeller, especially when sailing in areas where there are lobster pots. This simple device, a tight wire between the fin keel and the rudder skeg, may very slightly slow a boat down, but it certainly gives some peace of mind. Instead of the rigging screw, it might be preferable to use a tight multiple lashing to get the wire taut. The whole affair should be painted with antifouling, but if a rigging screw is used its threads should be heavily greased.

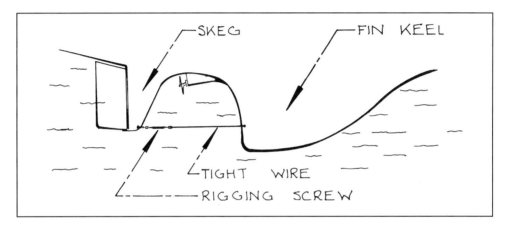

Rowlock improvements

Rowlocks have so many disadvantages. They tend to let oars jump out, usually in a rough sea, they tend to fall overboard, or if the boat is upturned they fall out of the boat and get lost.

These troubles can all be cured if two small holes are drilled, one at each end of the socket arms. Through these holes a piece of light Terylene line about ⅛ inch (3 mm) diameter is passed. The line is knotted just aft of the aft arm and then carried down and secured round a thwart. This line will prevent an oar jumping out of the rowlock, and if the line is kept just the right degree of tightness it will not restrict rowing but will prevent the rowlock from coming out of its hole by accident. The line is slackened slightly to lift the rowlock out of its socket. However, the end is still kept well secured so that if the dinghy is being towed and it capsizes, the rowlocks are not lost overboard.

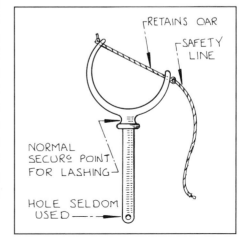

New life for an old boat

A heavily-used fibreglass boat tends to need repainting between her ninth and twelfth years. But repainting alone is not enough to give a boat a new lease of life. She may need a full re-fit and this sketch shows some of the things which can be done, often at no great expense. For instance, galvanising is surprisingly cheap, especially if a lot of fittings are sent all in one batch.

Sheets and halliards can sometimes be turned end for end. Meanwhile, the deck can be covered with one of the various sheathing materials or even teak to hide chips, chafes and scratches or discoloured fibreglass. A full covering of teak is expensive, but selected areas may be sheathed over and this will improve the appearance of the boat a great deal, provided the work is carefully done.

At the same time important fittings like the chain-plates, bilge pump, reefing gear, goose-neck, halliard sheaves and so on will need replacing or repairing or perhaps just a little modification.

Other items can be given an extra lease of life by local repairs. For instance, cushions tend to wear at the corners, so new corners can be stitched over or just occasionally the port cushion can be inverted and put upside down on the starb'd side and vice versa.

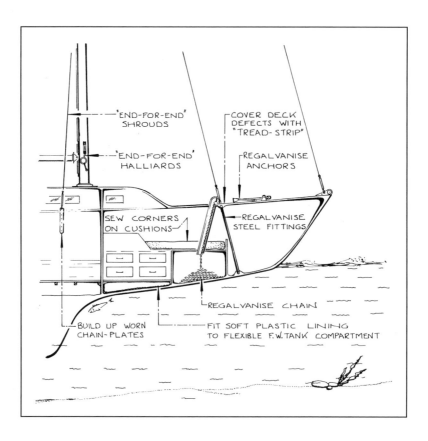

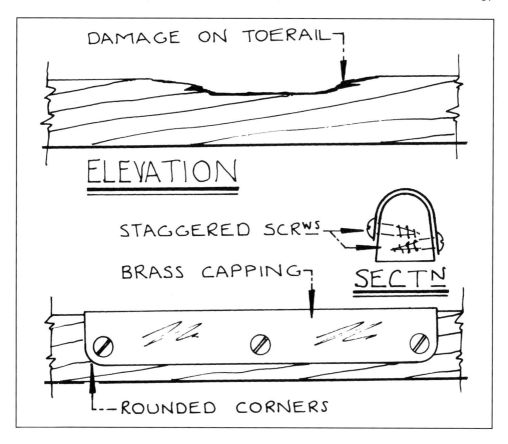

Toerail repair

Mending a toerail which is made of wood or fibreglass can be difficult. Sometimes the damage can be disguised by putting a brass or a stainless steel plate over the damage. The plate has to be thin enough to bend tightly round the toerail and it should have fastenings at least every 4 inches (100 mm) along each side.

In some cases this will be a temporary repair but it can be a permanent one if carefully done. Toerails tend to get damaged where they are vulnerable and the metal plate may act as a guard against future damage.

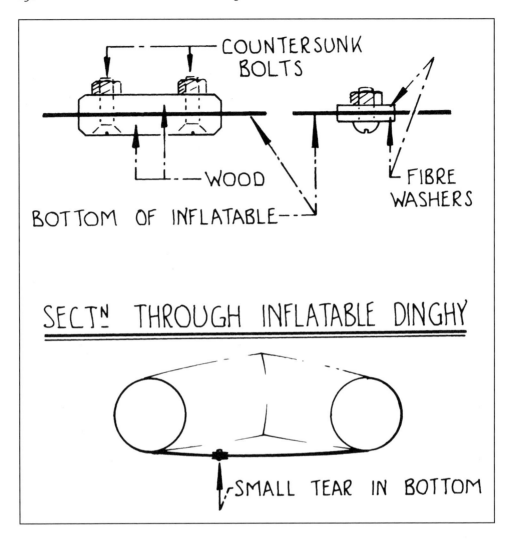

Temporary repairs to an inflatable dinghy

If the bottom of an inflatable dinghy is torn, a reasonable repair can be carried out without sending the boat to the manufacturers. A wood pad outside, with a matching one on the inside bolted through over a small tear, and properly bedded in place will prevent water getting in. If the tear is quite tiny it may be sufficient to put a single bolt with fibre washers each side through the bottom of the boat. Naturally this technique cannot be used if there is a leak in one of the inflated compartments.

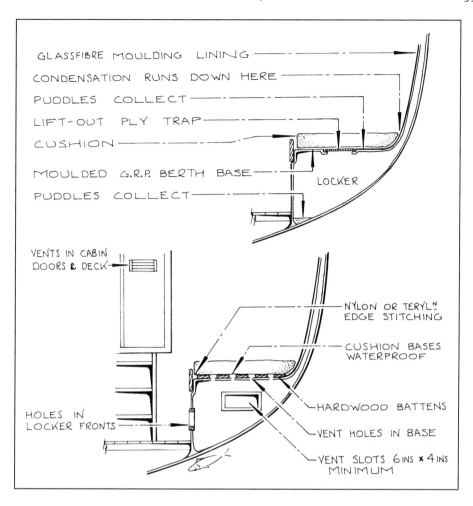

GLASSFIBRE MOULDING LINING
CONDENSATION RUNS DOWN HERE
PUDDLES COLLECT
LIFT-OUT PLY TRAP
CUSHION
MOULDED G.R.P. BERTH BASE
LOCKER
PUDDLES COLLECT

VENTS IN CABIN DOORS & DECK
NYLON OR TERYL." EDGE STITCHING
CUSHION BASES WATERPROOF
HARDWOOD BATTENS
HOLES IN LOCKER FRONTS
VENT HOLES IN BASE
VENT SLOTS 6 INS × 4 INS MINIMUM

Coping with condensation

The top sketch shows a typical settee berth in a fibreglass boat. Moisture tends to run down the inside of the moulded lining and collect beneath the cushion. Drips through the locker lid accumulate in the bottom of the locker and more condensation inside the hull runs down to collect in an ever increasing pool of water. To get over this, there should be a good draught through each locker. To achieve a draught there must be at least two slots in each enclosed space. Holes 1 inch (25 mm) in diameter are not big enough, especially when there are only gentle breezes passing through the boat.

The bottoms of all cushions should be raised above the fibreglass moulding with wood battens. In addition, each cushion should have a rot-proof leathercloth base which must not be stitched with common cotton because this soon rots when it is damp for any length of time.

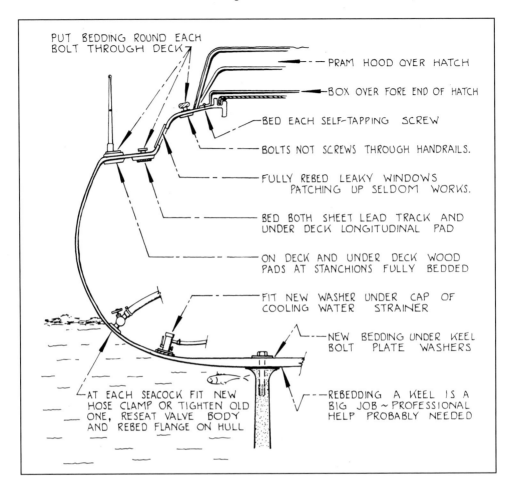

PUT BEDDING ROUND EACH
BOLT THROUGH DECK

PRAM HOOD OVER HATCH

BOX OVER FORE END OF HATCH

BED EACH SELF-TAPPING SCREW

BOLTS NOT SCREWS THROUGH HANDRAILS.

FULLY REBED LEAKY WINDOWS
PATCHING UP SELDOM WORKS.

BED BOTH SHEET LEAD TRACK AND
UNDER DECK LONGITUDINAL PAD

ON DECK AND UNDER DECK WOOD
PADS AT STANCHIONS FULLY BEDDED

FIT NEW WASHER UNDER CAP OF
COOLING WATER STRAINER

NEW BEDDING UNDER KEEL
BOLT PLATE WASHERS

AT EACH SEACOCK FIT NEW
HOSE CLAMP OR TIGHTEN OLD
ONE, RESEAT VALVE BODY
AND REBED FLANGE ON HULL

REBEDDING A KEEL IS A
BIG JOB ~ PROFESSIONAL
HELP PROBABLY NEEDED

Keeping the water out

During the course of a year some boats seem to let in water in mysterious ways. The bilge needs pumping every few days, yet there is no clear obvious leak through which water trickles like a merry gurgling brook. If a boat is always wet inside, it may be difficult to find out just where the water is coming from and the best plan may be to reseal all potential leaks. Certainly when taking over an old boat which has been wet inside, or before setting off on a long voyage, all potential leaks should be hunted down and stopped. Most jobs are quite simple and can be done even by an amateur with limited experience. Seacocks and keel bolts are more difficult and here professional help is often the best thing.

Hatches need special treatment, since they may leak when closed or when open. They should be tested when closed by turning a hose onto them, with an observer inside the cabin armed with a good flashlight to spot places where the water seeps in. To keep spray and rain out of the boat a pram hood over both the main and possibly even the fore hatch is well worth fitting on any cruising yacht.

NOTES

SKETCHES AND MEMOS

RESOURCES

CITY GUIDE DIRECTORY

A
Anchovies & Olives 032
1550 15th Avenue
T 206 838 8080
www.ethanstowellrestaurants.com
Area 51 084
401 E Pine Street
T 206 568 4782
www.area51seattle.com

B
Banya 5 088
217 9th Avenue N
T 206 262 1234
www.banya5.com
Barre3 091
1404 12th Avenue
T 206 257 1694
Seattle
1000 NW Marshall Street
Portland
Oregon
T 503 206 8308
www.barre3.com
Bastille 046
5307 NW Ballard Avenue
T 206 453 5014
www.bastilleseattle.com
Beast 097
5425 30th Avenue NE
Portland
Oregon
T 503 841 6968
www.beastpdx.com
Blackbird 082
5410 22nd Avenue NW
T 206 547 2524
www.blackbirdballard.com

Boat Street Café 030
3131 Western Avenue
T 206 632 4602
www.boatstreetcafe.com

C
Caffé Vita 032
1005 E Pike Street
T 206 709 4440
www.caffevita.com
Canlis 047
2576 N Aurora Avenue
T 206 283 3313
www.canlis.com
Central Library 060
1000 4th Avenue
T 206 386 4636
www.spl.org
Chapel of Saint Ignatius 057
901 12th Avenue
T 206 296 5587
www.seattleu.edu/
missionministry/chapel
Colman Pool 089
8603 SW Fauntleroy Way
T 206 684 7494
www.seattle.gov
Columbia Center 015
701 5th Avenue
T 206 386 5151
The Confectional 012
Pike Place Market
1st Avenue/Pike Street
T 206 282 4422
www.theconfectional.com
The Corson Building 036
5609 S Corson Avenue
T 206 762 3330
www.thecorsonbuilding.com

The Crumpet Shop 012
Pike Place Market
1st Avenue/Pike Street
T 206 682 1598
Cupcake Royale 048
1111 E Pike Street
T 206 883 7656
www.cupcakeroyale.com
Curtis Steiner 074
5349 NW Ballard Avenue
T 206 297 7116
www.curtissteiner.com

D
Dahlia 018
2001 4th Avenue
T 206 441 4540
www.tomdouglas.com
Delancey 033
1415 70th Street NW
T 206 838 1960
www.delanceyseattle.com
Departure 097
525 SW Morrison Street
Portland
Oregon
T 503 802 5370
www.departureportland.com
Dutch Bike Co 025
4741 NW Ballard Avenue
T 206 789 1678
www.dutchbikeseattle.com

E
Experience Music Project 070
325 5th Avenue N
T 206 770 2700
www.empmuseum.org

F
Far 4 073
1020 1st Avenue
T 206 621 8831
www.far4.net
The Field House 080
5465 NW Leary Avenue
www.blackbirdballard.com
First Presbyterian Church 068
1013 8th Avenue
T 206 624 0644
www.firstpres.org
Four Seasons Spa 090
Four Seasons
99 Union Street
T 206 749 7077
www.fourseasons.com/seattle/spa
Frye Art Museum 062
704 Terry Avenue
T 206 622 9250
www.fryemuseum.org

G
Gorge Amphitheatre 102
754 NW Silica Road
George
T 509 785 6262
Graypants 054
3320 1st Avenue S
T 206 420 3912
www.graypants.com

H
Henry Art Gallery 026
15th Avenue NE/41st Street
T 206 543 2280
www.henryart.org
The Hideout 031
1005 Boren Avenue
T 206 903 8480
www.hideoutseattle.com

Hot Cakes 045
T 206 412 8166
www.autumnmartin.com

Hub & Bespoke 087
513 36th Street N
T 206 547 5730
www.hubandbespoke.com

J

Jack Straw 078
1117 1st Avenue
T 206 462 6236
www.jstraw.com

K

Knew Gardens 056
1422 34th Avenue
T 206 323 0111
www.domesticarchitecture.com

L

Lighthouse Roasters 042
400 43rd Street N
T 206 634 3140
www.lighthouseroasters.com

Little Bird 097
219 6th Avenue SW
Portland
Oregon
T 503 688 5952
www.littlebirdbistro.com

Lola 018
2000 4th Avenue
T 206 441 1430
www.tomdouglas.com

M

Marigold & Mint 072
1531 Melrose Avenue
T 206 682 3111
www.marigoldandmint.com

Mighty-O 045
2110 55th Street N
T 206 547 0335
www.mightyo.com

Molly Moon's 052
917 E Pine Street
T 206 708 7947
1622 45th Street N
T 206 547 5105
108 Pine Street
T 206 443 3900
1408 34th Avenue
www.mollymoonicecream.com

N

Neumos 032
925 E Pike Street
T 206 709 9467
www.neumos.com

Nube Green 077
921 E Pine Sreet
T 206 402 4515
www.nubegreen.com

O

Olympic Sculpture Park 064
2901 Western Avenue
T 206 654 3100
www.seattleartmuseum.org/visit/osp

Osteria La Spiga 038
1429 12th Avenue
T 206 323 8881
www.laspiga.com

P

Pacific Science Center 066
200 2nd Avenue N
T 206 443 2001
www.pacificsciencecenter.org
Pettirosso 054
1101 E Pike Street
T 206 323 4830
Le Pigeon 097
738 E Burnside Street
Portland
Oregon
T 503 546 8796
www.lepigeon.com
Pike Place Market 012
1st Avenue/Pike Street
T 206 682 7453
www.pikeplacemarket.org
Poquitos 050
1000 E Pike Street
T 206 453 4216
www.vivapoquitos.com
Portland Building 097
1221 4th Avenue SW
Portland
Oregon

Q

Qwest Field 092
800 S Occidental Avenue
T 206 381 7500
www.qwestfield.com

R

Rainier Tower 014
1301 5th Avenue
Revel 040
403 36th Street N
T 206 547 2040
www.revelseattle.com

Rock Box 032
1603 Nagle Place
T 206 302 7625
www.rockboxseattle.com

S

Safeco Field 092
1250 1st Avenue S
T 206 346 4001
www.mariners.mlb.com
Salumi 054
309 3rd Avenue S
T 206 621 8772
www.salumicuredmeats.com
Seattle Art Museum 028
1300 1st Avenue
T 206 654 3100
www.seattleartmuseum.org
Sitka & Spruce 034
1531 E Melrose Avenue
T 206 324 0662
www.sitkaandspruce.com
Skillet Diner 043
1400 E Union Street
T 206 420 7297
www.skilletstreetfood.com
Space Needle 013
219 4th Avenue
T 206 905 2100
www.spaceneedle.com
Spur Gastropub 041
113 Blanchard Street
T 206 728 6706
www.spurseattle.com
Staple & Fancy 051
4739 Ballard Avenue
T 206 789 1200
www.ethanstowellrestaurants.com

Stumptown Coffee Roasters 044
1115 12th Avenue
T 206 323 1544
616 E Pine Street
T 206 329 0115
www.stumptowncoffee.com
Sugar Pill 086
900 E Pine Street
T 206 322 7455
www.sugarpillseattle.com
Sun Liquor Distillery 037
514 E Pike Street
T 206 720 1600
www.sunliquor.com

T
20twenty 087
5208 Ballard Avenue
T 206 706 0969
www.twentytwentyballard.blogspot.com
Tavern Law 041
1406 12th Avenue
T 206 322 9734
www.tavernlaw.com
Tavolàta 016
2323 2nd Avenue
T 206 838 8008
www.ethanstowellrestaurants.com

U
Urban Yoga 094
1900 4th Avenue
T 206 420 0222
www.urbanyogaspa.com

V
Velocity 076
251 N Yale Avenue
T 206 749 9575
www.velocityartanddesign.com

W
The Walrus and the Carpenter 030
4743 Ballard Avenue
T 206 395 9227
www.thewalrusbar.com
Western Bridge 077
3412 4th Avenue S
T 206 838 7444
www.westernbridge.org
Wheelhouse Coffee 042
2113 Westlake Avenue
T 206 467 0160
www.wheelhousecoffee.com
The Willows Inn 096
2579 West Shore Drive
Lummi Island
T 360 758 2620
www.willows-inn.com

HOTELS
ADDRESSES AND ROOM RATES

Ace Hotel Portland 097
Room rates:
double, from, $165;
Superior Deluxe Room, $275
1022 SW Stark Street
Portland
Oregon
T 503 228 2277
www.acehotel.com/portland

Ace Hotel Seattle 022
Room rates:
double, from $98;
Standard, $109
2423 1st Avenue
T 206 448 4721
www.acehotel.com/seattle

Hotel Andra 018
Room rates:
double, from £189;
Lux Suite, $279
2000 4th Avenue
T 206 448 8600
www.hotelandra.com

Cave B Inn & Spa 102
Room rates:
double, from $255
344 NW Silica Road
Quincy
T 888 785 2283
www.sagecliffe.com

Four Seasons 021
Room rates:
double, from $315;
Bay View Room, $595;
Presidential Suite, $5,000
99 Union Street
T 206 749 7000
www.fourseasons.com/seattle

Inn at the Market 016
Room rates:
double, from $255
86 Pine Street
T 206 443 3600
www.innatthemarket.com

The Maxwell Hotel 016
Room rates:
double, from $179
300 Roy Street
T 206 286 0629
www.themaxwellhotel.com

Hotel 1000 017
Room rates:
double, from $189;
Luxe, $425;
Grand Luxe, $999;
Grand Suite, $5,000
1000 1st Avenue
T 206 957 1000
www.hotel1000seattle.com

Rolling Huts 100
Rates:
from $125
18381 Highway 20
Winthrop
T 509 996 4442
www.rollinghuts.com

Sorrento Hotel 016
Room rates:
double, from $179
900 Madison Street
T 206 622 6400
www.hotelsorrento.com

W 020
Room rates:
double, from $269;
Cool Corner Room, $399;
Extreme Wow Suite, $1,900
1112 4th Avenue
T 206 264 6000
www.starwoodhotels.com

WALLPAPER* CITY GUIDES

Executive Editor
Rachael Moloney

Author
Eva Hagberg

Art Director
Loran Stosskopf

Art Editor
Eriko Shimazaki
Designer
Mayumi Hashimoto
Map Illustrator
Russell Bell

Photography Editor
Sophie Corben
Photography Assistant
Nabil Butt

Chief Sub-Editor
Nick Mee
Sub-Editors
Emily Brooks
Simon Crook
Greg Hughes

Editorial Assistant
Emma Harrison

Intern
Candace Rardon

**Wallpaper* Group
Editor-in-Chief**
Tony Chambers
Publishing Director
Gord Ray
Managing Editor
Jessica Diamond

Contributor
Megan A Vrolijk

Wallpaper* ® is a
registered trademark
of IPC Media Limited

First published 2012

All prices are correct at
the time of going to press,
but are subject to change.

Printed in China

PHAIDON

Phaidon Press Limited
Regent's Wharf
All Saints Street
London N1 9PA

Phaidon Press Inc
180 Varick Street
New York, NY 10014

Phaidon® is a registered
trademark of Phaidon
Press Limited

www.phaidon.com

A CIP Catalogue record for
this book is available from
the British Library.

© 2011 IPC Media Limited

ISBN 978 0 7148 6296 5

PHOTOGRAPHERS

Tim Bies/Olson Kundig Architects
Rolling Huts, p100, p101

DK/Alamy
Portland Building, p097

Timothy Hursley
Qwest Field, pp092-093

Andrea Johnson
Cave B Inn & Spa, pp102-103

Lara Swimmer
Seattle city view, inside front cover
I-5, pp010-011
Pike Place Market, p012
Space Needle, p013
Rainier Tower, p014
Columbia Center, p015
Hotel 1000, p017
Hotel Andra, p018, p019
W, p020
Four Seasons, p021
Ace Hotel, p022, p023
Dutch Bike Co, p025
Henry Art Gallery, p026, p027
Seattle Art Museum, p029
The Walrus and the Carpenter, p030
The Hideout, p031
Delancey, p033
Sitka & Spruce, pp034-035
The Corson Building, p036
Sun Liquor Distillery, p037

Osteria La Spiga, pp038-039
Revel, p040
Tavern Law, p041
Wheelhouse Coffee, p042
Skillet Diner, p043
Stumptown Coffee Roasters, pp044-045
Bastille, p046
Canlis, p047
Cupcake Royale, pp048-049
Poquitos, p050
Staple & Fancy, p051
Molly Moon's, pp052-053
Seth Grizzle, p055
Chapel of Saint Ignatius, p057, pp058-059
Central Library, pp060-061
Frye Art Museum, p062, p063
Olympic Sculpture Park, pp064-065
Pacific Science Center, pp066-067
First Presbyterian Church, p068, p069
Experience Music Project, pp070-071
Far 4, p073
Curtis Steiner, pp074-075
Velocity, p076
Nube Green, p077
Jack Straw, pp078-079
The Field House, pp080-081

Blackbird, p082
Area 51, pp084-085
Sugar Pill, p086
Hub & Bespoke, p087
Colman Pool, p089
Four Seasons Spa, p090
Barre3, p091
Urban Yoga, pp094-095

SEATTLE
A COLOUR-CODED GUIDE TO THE HOT 'HOODS

BALLARD
Hipsters have been steadily gravitating to this area's eateries and artsy ateliers

CAPITOL HILL
Eat, drink, party and get your caffeine kicks in the city's hotbed of urban life

FREMONT
Explore the offbeat charms of this quirky area, starting at its organic chocolate factory

SEATTLE CENTER/BELLTOWN
Extraordinary architecture meets semi-industrial frontier in these adjacent areas

DOWNTOWN
Skimming the waterfront are Seattle's high-rise cluster and most luxurious hotels

UNIVERSITY DISTRICT
Student-focused culture gives this leafy part of town its energetic, experimental vibe

For a full description of each neighbourhood, see the Introduction.
Featured venues are colour-coded, according to the district in which they are located.